WHERE WAS GOD?

WHERE WAS GOD?

faith in times of trouble

KIRA TALERICO

Copyright © 2024 by Kira Talerico

All rights reserved. This book or any portion thereof may not be reproduced or used in any manner whatsoever without the express written permission of the publisher except for the use of brief quotations in a book review.

Printed in the United States of America

First Printing, 2024

Paperback ISBN: 979-8-3305-1747-3
eBook ISBN: 979-8-3305-1754-1

Jesus Beside Me Publishing
Mount Pleasant, SC 29466

Scripture Quotations are from the Holy Bible, NIV
www.amazon.com/WherewasGod

To my dear friend, Jesus. I will love you until the day I am back in your presence. Until then, I will seek your face.

CONTENTS

Chapter 1	Just Another Monday	1
Chapter 2	Oh. My. Goodness	11
Chapter 3	The PICU	26

BEFORE		**29**
Chapter 4	A Talerico History	31
Chapter 5	A Trial Run	44
Chapter 6	I Can Do Hard Things	49
Chapter 7	Vinny's A Rockstar	54
Chapter 8	CODE BLUE	71
Chapter 9	When Mary Wept	82
Chapter 10	Paul, Mary, and Martha	98
Chapter 11	Out Of My Hands	135

AFTER		**157**
Chapter 12	A Thorn In My Side	159
Chapter 13	Unanswerable Questions	171
Chapter 14	Be Bold	190
Chapter 15	A Long Deep Breath	197
Chapter 16	Why? Where? What if?	205
Chapter 17	Call Me Mara	217
Chapter 18	Patient Endurance	225
Chapter 19	Jesus Beside Us	236

Epilogue	243
What Now?	249
Bible Verses for Grief and Suffering	255
Acknowledgments	267
References	269

CHAPTER 1

JUST ANOTHER MONDAY

Why do bad things happen? It's the question we all ask when times get hard. Why God? How could you let this happen? Where are you??? Don't you hear me? But I prayed! I prayed hard! I was on my knees … and where were you? So continues the pleas of a broken heart.

It was just another Monday. I was getting ready to send my two wonderful boys to school when my oldest, Vinny, age nine, mentioned he had a belly ache and wasn't feeling well. I took his temperature just in case, post-Covid world and all, and it was a low but notable 99.3. This wasn't the first Monday with the same symptoms. In fact, he had missed eight of his third grade Mondays so far. I had taken him to the pediatrician to see if there were any issues and after checking him out, they didn't find anything alarming. They decided something must be happening on Mondays that was causing his stomach to hurt. As any mom knows, when your kid is sick they show it physically. Every time it happened, and I allowed him to stay home from school, my vivacious little rockstar was perfectly fine and bouncing off the couch by 10 a.m.! We decided maybe it was anxiety related and he started seeing the school counselor just to make sure there wasn't something happening on Mondays that was causing him stress.

This particular Monday though, the stomach pain and low-grade fever did not recede. In fact, at 10 p.m. that night, he woke up screaming in pain. For a nine-year-old to wake up in pain, in the middle of the night, from a dead sleep is alarming. My husband Chris and I rushed to his room. He said his side hurt, through clenched teeth and closed eyes. "Is it bad enough to go to the emergency room?" I asked. "Maybe," was his strained reply. This was distressing to us because he wasn't really one to complain. We gave him some Tums, just in case it was something easily remedied. We decided if he didn't fall asleep from relief within twenty minutes, we would bring him to the emergency room. Twenty minutes later, he was sleeping soundly. We chose to address it in the morning if he was still feeling the pain.

CHAPTER 1

JUST ANOTHER MONDAY

Why do bad things happen? It's the question we all ask when times get hard. Why God? How could you let this happen? Where are you??? Don't you hear me? But I prayed! I prayed hard! I was on my knees … and where were you? So continues the pleas of a broken heart.

It was just another Monday. I was getting ready to send my two wonderful boys to school when my oldest, Vinny, age nine, mentioned he had a belly ache and wasn't feeling well. I took his temperature just in case, post-Covid world and all, and it was a low but notable 99.3. This wasn't the first Monday with the same symptoms. In fact, he had missed eight of his third grade Mondays so far. I had taken him to the pediatrician to see if there were any issues and after checking him out, they didn't find anything alarming. They decided something must be happening on Mondays that was causing his stomach to hurt. As any mom knows, when your kid is sick they show it physically. Every time it happened, and I allowed him to stay home from school, my vivacious little rockstar was perfectly fine and bouncing off the couch by 10 a.m.! We decided maybe it was anxiety related and he started seeing the school counselor just to make sure there wasn't something happening on Mondays that was causing him stress.

This particular Monday though, the stomach pain and low-grade fever did not recede. In fact, at 10 p.m. that night, he woke up screaming in pain. For a nine-year-old to wake up in pain, in the middle of the night, from a dead sleep is alarming. My husband Chris and I rushed to his room. He said his side hurt, through clenched teeth and closed eyes. "Is it bad enough to go to the emergency room?" I asked. "Maybe," was his strained reply. This was distressing to us because he wasn't really one to complain. We gave him some Tums, just in case it was something easily remedied. We decided if he didn't fall asleep from relief within twenty minutes, we would bring him to the emergency room. Twenty minutes later, he was sleeping soundly. We chose to address it in the morning if he was still feeling the pain.

The next morning, when he woke up I asked, "How is your stomach feeling today?" "The same," he replied quietly. I called the pediatrician and they told me to take him to the local ER to make sure he didn't have an appendicitis. After getting my youngest, Chase, age seven, off to school, we drove Vinny to the neighborhood emergency room. This particular hospital was less than ten minutes from home and since Vinny was no longer crying out in pain, we weren't sure how "emergency" the situation was. We just felt that something wasn't right; mother's intuition and all. By the way, if anyone, regardless of their "professional position," tells you that as a parent your intuition is incorrect, get a second opinion. More on that later.

Once we arrived at the hospital, we were told only one adult was allowed in with him because of Covid rules. When we were in the exam room I explained what Vinny's symptoms were to the doctor. He examined the approximate location of his appendix and said he saw no signs of appendicitis and that it was just a stomach bug. He advised that we wait it out.

This did not sit right with me. For one, I'm a mom of two boys. We've had PLENTY of stomach bugs and I am well aware of the symptoms! I would not be in the ER if I thought it was a stomach bug. I politely asked the doctor if he was sure, because Vinny described it as a pain different than the kind you get with a stomach virus. The fact that it had woken him from a dead sleep was worrisome to me. The doctor threw his hands up in the air as if I should dare question him. He told me if I didn't agree with his assessment, that I should go somewhere else, and that he "didn't have the right equipment to test a child anyways." I won't lie, this made me feel like a complete fool. Of course, mothers overreact. The doctor assured me it was nothing and that I should trust that Vinny would start vomiting soon. No labs or tests were done beyond feeling his abdomen. Even the nurse assured me it was a stomach bug as she had seen eight other cases just that week. Relieved that it was not an emergency appendicitis, we took Vinny home.

Each day after that, his fever rose by one degree. On Thursday I took him to his pediatrician to have him looked at again. His fever was now holding steady at 102 and the pain in his stomach was still present with no other classic signs of a stomach virus. He was pale and lethargic. She examined him briefly and said, "Well if the ER didn't find anything serious then I am sure they are right about the stomach virus. Wait it out a few more days and just watch for dehydration." On Friday, Vinny's temperature rose to 103. He was weak and pallid with bags under his eyes and

I thought maybe he was getting dehydrated, although I had seen him drinking water. I was giving him hydration packets and doing everything I could to treat the fever. As we all know, fevers are a good thing and the body's sign of fighting an infection. I have heard this countless times in my nine years as a mom. "Don't worry mom, fevers are normal," the doctors would say, "He'll be just fine."

I was able to get him and his brother outside for some fresh air and to sit on the swings out back for a bit. He had a tired smile on his face and I could see he had no energy. After about ten minutes, he slowly walked inside and I began to worry.

Late at night on Friday his fever climbed to 104. I administered his pain meds and the fever wouldn't budge. I gave them to him again an hour later and still no movement. We contemplated taking him to the ER again but two doctors had just told us to "wait it out." I remembered hearing that if a temperature is no longer responding to medication, it's time to go to the hospital. My husband called a friend of ours who is a pharmacist and he said if it was one of his daughters, he'd be on his way to the children's hospital immediately.

After feeling blown off by the local ER and again by the pediatrician, we decided to bypass them and go straight to the children's hospital in downtown Charleston, South Carolina. Because of the Covid restrictions and also having another sleeping child at home, we thought I should just take Vinny myself since they would probably only let one of us in anyway. Chris carried him to the car. At this point it was around 10 p.m. on Friday and Vinny was getting so lethargic he could barely hold his head up, let alone stand and walk to the car. Seeing him like this started a slow panic in me as he had only seemed tired until now.

As I was driving the thirty minutes it took to get to the hospital, I kept trying to talk to him. He was worried as well and was having a hard time sitting up straight. He was telling me that he was scared because, "When you are dehydrated, they insert an IV to get fluids into your body." He knew the IV would hurt and he really didn't want one. I tried to calmly tell him that if they had to do an IV, it would help him get the fluids he needed to get better, that it would be quick and I would be there, right by his side.

I drove down the empty, dark highway with the lights streaming by. It was eerily quiet and felt like the longest drive of my life. I was trying to get there as fast as I could without driving recklessly. At one point he whimpered, "Hurry Mom." This moment still brings tears to my eyes and a tremor in my hands. For a brave, funny, nine-year-old boy with a type-A personality to ask me to hurry to the ER, I knew he wasn't feeling good. Still, I just thought whatever bug was in him had made him severely dehydrated, even though I was doing everything I knew to keep that from happening. In hindsight, I should have called an ambulance, but I didn't know how dire the situation was until that moment.

When we pulled up to the ER, I left my car in the drive-up lane and Vinny and I walked inside. There were about twenty stairs to get up to the main entrance desk from the emergency doors. I asked him if he wanted me to carry him or if he could make it up himself. Let me preface this by saying I am 5'3" and relatively small in stature. My son is almost as tall as me and if he needed me to, I could carry him piggyback style with his feet dangling at my knees. But he said he could make it. As we slowly climbed the stairs, I held onto him as he grasped the bannister. Step by anxious step we made it up the stairs and to the check-in desk.

At that moment, the receptionist asked, "How can I help you?" and with a whoosh of air Vinny collapsed beside me. I caught him in my arms but he had gone completely unconscious. Panic gripped me. The receptionist didn't seem fazed enough for my liking so I screamed for someone to help us and two or three nurses burst through the waiting room doors. One of them scooped him up in their arms as if he was only ten pounds and said, "Follow me, Mom."

At this point I was shaking. I did not know what was going on. Why had he collapsed? Could he be THAT dehydrated? I followed behind the nurses with tears quietly streaming down my face as we passed the quiet ER rooms. They rushed us to his designated room and eight doctors and nurses swarmed in. They put a stool next to his bed and told me to sit by his side while the nurses did what they do best. It was like choreographed chaos as some called out orders. Someone immediately put in an IV, hooked up monitors and took his temperature. A nurse was kneeling on the floor flushing Vinny's IV with fluids, three or four large syringes full. At that moment I breathed a sigh of relief that he was getting the fluids he needed. He was unconscious still and, remembering our conversation in the car, I was glad he wouldn't feel the IV he was so concerned about. His fever was still a staggering 104 degrees. They were not able to give him any more fever medication because I had already given him the max dosage for now, since I administered it back-to-back.

While all of this was happening at a lightning speed, a woman in a white coat came up beside me. As she was quickly looking him over she was firing questions at me. What brought this on? What were his symptoms? How long has it been? She said, "Does he look pale to you, Mom?" I said, "Of course he's pale, he's running 104 fever and it's been a week!" She followed with, "Mom, are these bruises on his legs normal?"

Now let me tell you. In hindsight, I should have caught that question. But in my mind, we were there for dehydration. I figured that was why he passed out and every doctor before that warned me it could happen. My response was, "He's a nine-year-old boy who does wild flips on our trampoline, plays soccer, and runs around all day barefoot. So yes, bruises on his legs are QUITE normal!"

Little did I know, the doctors had a clear idea of what could be the cause of his desperate condition. As he regained consciousness, they cleared the room, running their tests and waiting for the results. He was weak but awake and I explained where we were and what had happened. I even pointed out how timely it was for him to lose consciousness because he didn't have to feel the IV needle! He laughed weakly at that and said he didn't feel it at all. It was probably thirty minutes before the doctors came back into the room. I thought it was very fast considering every other time I have been in a hospital, test results seem to take hours, if not days. He had fallen back asleep given it was past 11 p.m. and he was still burning up.

When the two doctors walked in, they closed the clear glass sliding door behind them and slowly pulled up two chairs. I was already concerned but this was bad. What would they have to tell me that was so serious? So much so that they would carefully sit down and speak in soft, kind words.

"Mom, Vinny has leukemia."

CHAPTER 2

OH. MY. GOODNESS.

Silence. I sat there staring blankly at the doctors in blatant denial. I checked to see if Vinny was still asleep before I spoke. In disbelief I said, "No, you must have that wrong. We are here for dehydration. He doesn't have cancer." The room was quiet and it was the middle of the night so the fluorescent lights were glowing with a low hum.

"Based on the tests we ran, we are pretty sure he has leukemia," said the main doctor. I was baffled. It seemed like I couldn't quite grasp what they were saying.

"So are you telling me you "think" he has cancer, or you know it's cancer?" I replied.

"We are 99 percent sure. But oncology will be here around 3 a.m. to confirm and discuss this with you further."

I guess I must have looked like a deer in headlights because suddenly she said, "Can I give you a hug? It looks like you may need one." Slowly we stood up and she embraced me in a gentle hug. I was completely confused and still VERY much disbelieving the doctors' words. He was sick but not like THAT. How could we go from a stomach bug to, what did she say? Cancer? The oncology doctors were already alerted and coming down at 3 a.m. to talk to me? This is crazy. They'll confirm it's a mistake for sure.

I didn't know it then, but I would never forget that ER doctor. I never got her name but later I would imagine what a horrible shift that was for her. To have that conversation. To give that diagnosis to a completely blindsided parent of a little boy when she thought he had a stomach bug. The compassion and care she had in her voice will, like many other moments, be burned into my memories.

As soon as they left, I jumped into the small, private bathroom attached to Vinny's room. I called my husband and told him what I had just heard. He was just as shocked and somewhat disbelieving as I was. I needed him there with me. The nurses said that it would be no problem for both of us to be in the hospital and that he should get there as soon as he could. Next, I called one of our closest friends and neighbor, Faye. As she answered the phone I whispered, "they said it's leukemia." Faye was well aware of the previous week and how Vinny had been feeling. I will never forget her shouting into the phone, "What??? No Kira, please get a second opinion, that's ridiculous. He was just fine last week!" Like me, she couldn't believe their diagnosis and wouldn't even think twice that they were correct because it was so outlandish.

Faye and Justin are our twin family. They live just down the street, are the same age as us, and our children are the same age as theirs. They are the BEST of friends. We had literally just spent the weekend in Myrtle Beach together where the kids were swimming and having a great time before Vinny started feeling ill. There was no hint that something was wrong. My boys know Faye and Justin like a second family. For the last eight years we spent holidays, birthdays, and most regular days in between together.

I relayed to her what the doctors said. After seeing his pale demeanor and the bruises on his legs the doctors tested his blood. His white blood cell count was over 80,000. For those who don't have a close personal relationship with white blood cells, 5,000–10,000 is what a healthy child should have. I would soon learn that his bone marrow was pumping out cancerous white blood cells at an alarming rate. Faye agreed to run over and grab Chase so that Chris could come to the hospital. Getting this news alone, well, sucks.

Next, I had to call my parents. I have to tell you that God had really set us up to be surrounded by love during this time. My parents, Leo and Sherry, were in the process of closing on their house in Florida so that they could move up to Charleston to be closer to us and watch the boys grow up. "Mainly for the boys," my mom lovingly jokes and I love it. We have always lived far from them, and this was the first time in my children's life that they would be close geographically. They had always wanted to be able to see the boys play sports, or at least through their high school years, but it worked out that they were able to move sooner. In fact, they had just been with us for a week right before Vinny got sick and they had planned to move up in three weeks' time.

I called my dad from that tiny bathroom at around one in the morning. Naturally he knew something was wrong based on the timing of my call. As soon as I told him what was happening, they jumped out of bed, packed a bag, and got in the car for the seven-hour trip back to us from their home in Florida.

Chris arrived at the hospital thirty minutes later. We sat quietly by Vinny's bed until 3 a.m. when a team of oncology doctors came to collect us. They brought us to a private, teeny tiny family room (or more accurately, a closet with chairs) which is never good, but I was glad Vinny wouldn't hear what they had to say. As one closed the door, the others confirmed that he did in fact have leukemia. His white blood cell count assured them of the diagnosis. They were going to rush his blood work to the lab for typing (determining which type of leukemia he had) but we would not find out the results until later the next day.

There are three types when it comes to childhood leukemia: the bad kind, the worse kind, and then the chronic version of the disease. Most kids have the bad kind called acute lymphoblastic leukemia (ALL). ALL has a 90 percent survival rate. This type is the most common in children and has an average outpatient treatment of one and a half years. The worse kind is called acute myeloid leukemia (AML). It has a survival rate of just 68 percent at five years and has an intensive six to seven month inpatient, around the clock treatment because of the aggressiveness of the cancer. Chronic myeloid leukemia (CML) is the rarest form, with only 2 percent being diagnosed, and has a survival rate of 60-80 percent after five years. They informed us that it was unlikely he would be diagnosed with CML so more than likely it was one of the first two.

At this point, I had to let go of the idea that this was some kind of mistake. As they told us what life would look like with a child battling leukemia, I realized things were going to be dramatically different from now on. He'd have to stop going to school because his immune system would be compromised and he would miss too much from either treatment anyways. He would have frequent chemotherapy treatments and definitely lose the hair he had worked so hard to grow out. (As a side note, my boy LOVED his hair longer. He refused to let me cut it and it was at the median length that he would have to sweep his neck to move his hair off of his eyes. It was one of his first choices as an individual to do something different than what his mom wanted.)

I don't exactly remember the specifics of the rest of the conversation because with every remark I sank further and further into my chair. After every change in lifestyle they mentioned I exclaimed, "Oh. My. Goodness." Louder and louder. My poor baby and what he would have to go through. Regardless of what type it was, everything was derailed. His whole existence. Vinny desperately loved his friends and playing soccer at lunchtime recess. We had booked our first family trip to Mexico months before and were supposed to leave the following Friday. He was beyond excited. We had watched all kinds of YouTube videos about the resort and what it would be like to stay there! All of that was about to be taken away, or rather traded for a neon yellow bag with the sticker "Caution: Poison" attached to it.

The next day I cried and cried. And cried some more. Silently, balled up in an uncomfortable hospital chair I wept as Vinny slept. We had been moved to a general admittance room as we waited for the test results of his blood work. Once we had the official diagnosis, they would send us to his permanent residence on the tenth floor: Hematology and Oncology. Vinny was awake and talking but still visibly VERY sick. His belly continued to hurt and we didn't have answers as to the cause for that yet. His fever was holding steady at 104 degrees and his cheeks were permanently flushed. They surrounded him with ice packs and popsicles to keep him cool while we waited in anticipation. The nurses brought up a gaming system, and as Vinny was a typical elementary school boy, that was a big hit. At this point we had not yet explained to him why we were still in the hospital. He was constantly asking when we could go home. He didn't understand why they were making him stay and he just wanted to lay in his own bed with his own pillow and blanket.

One of our newly dedicated oncology doctors, Dr. Paige, finally pulled me out of the room around noon to go over the results. One of the nurses stayed with Chris and Vinny to play video games and keep him occupied while we talked. We stood in the corner of the hallway as she told me that Vinny's diagnosis was the "worse" kind.

Acute myeloid leukemia, or AML, was the one with a survival rate of between 60-70 percent at five years. As all good doctors do, she assured me that these diagnoses come in waves and they had a few other patients on the floor with the exact same diagnosis. "Our oncology team is the best when it comes to our kiddos," she said, and she assured me they would do everything possible to get him treatment quickly because of the aggressiveness of this type of cancer. His numbers were climbing rapidly. His high fever was a symptom of the cancer alone and would not lessen by any means until the cancer was eradicated. AML also meant that instead of outpatient treatments, where he would get to sleep in his own bed, he would be admitted immediately and would undergo six to seven months of intense inpatient treatment at the hospital. He would only be able to go home on day thirty, for one night of each month, if his immune system could handle it. Because it was 2021 and Covid rules reigned supreme, he would be allowed no more than two visitors at the hospital. Chris and I were it. Once his stay was longer than twelve days inpatient, two more people could be added to the list. This meant no friends, no family, no outside world for almost seven months. I continued to cry for my baby. Quietly, privately, away from him. How could this be happening?

The plan was to get him up to floor ten as soon as a room became available later that day. This meant that I would have to wheel him up to the oncology unit and the first thing you see when the elevator doors open is the word oncology. Vinny is a very intelligent kid and would immediately wonder why he was on the cancer floor.

Can I tell you this was the worst conversation of my life? How do you tell your baby that he has cancer, especially when he's old enough to be terrified of the word?

A few weeks before all of this happened, we had been enjoying a show on Netflix about teen figure skaters as a family. The best friend of the main character happened to have been a recent survivor of childhood leukemia. This gave us a reference for him to look to. It's funny how sometimes God puts something in your life to soften the blow of a trial yet to come, a point of reference.

We were notified around 4:30 that a room had become available and the attendant would be taking us up soon. The time had come for us to tell Vinny the diagnosis before he saw the literal writing on the wall. As Chris and I sat on his bed, I explained that we were about to be moved to his real room. I told him that we wouldn't be leaving the hospital that night and he started to get upset. "Do we have to stay another night?" he asked. My chest squeezed as I told him it would be longer than that. "A week? Do I have to stay a whole week, Mom?" I didn't have the heart to tell him it would be six months at that point and I figured why make it worse so I settled with saying, "A month, Vinny, you have to stay a whole month." He shouted back worriedly, "BUT WHAT ABOUT MEXICO?? We're supposed to go on Friday!!" The innocence of that being one of his first thoughts was not lost on me. It sweetly broke my heart. "We won't be going to Mexico now, buddy," we told him. I said, "I have to tell you the name of what you have now, but it's hard." I had to pause to get up the courage to utter that earth-shattering word to my child. As I sat on his bed holding one of his hands and Chris kneeled at the bedside holding the other, I said, "Vinny, you have leukemia." He sat there, mouth open, tears welling in his eyes, with no words. I said, "Remember the girl on the show we were watching? She had leukemia too and she's just fine now." He slowly nodded his head in understanding but remained quiet and looked scared. I whispered, "Do you need a hug?" My kid is intensely independent but he silently shook his head yes. So the three of us hugged there for the seven seconds he would allow. The longest hug we had gotten from him in a while. When he pulled back I said, "Now, in a few minutes we will head upstairs to the cancer floor where you will start your treatments and your father and I will be there with you every step of the way. The three of us will do this together and at the end of your treatment we will all celebrate by going to Mexico." With a brave face he sucked up his tears and I chose to suck up mine too. I wouldn't cry again. I would be strong and resilient for my child as we prepared to move to the tenth floor.

We were moved up to a permanent room on the highest level and Vinny continued to get weaker and weaker. The pain in his stomach was becoming too much to bear so they decided to medicate him with the good stuff. He was drastically more comfortable after that, but as the day progressed his belly became distended. He was retaining large amounts of fluid and whatever was causing him pain in the abdomen was only getting worse. He was so weak that anytime he would try to stand, even just for a moment, he would practically lose consciousness and fall back onto the bed as his blood pressure plummeted. Without being able to move on his own, expelling the fluid would be difficult. My husband spent the morning at Vinny's side trying to joke with him. They played games while I ran home to get us some personal items. I had been in the same clothes for days now and needed a shower. While I was gone, they were able to have a video chat with Chris's parents, Jim and Georgeann, over the phone. It was a much needed and uplifting conversation.

Because Vinny was going to be in the hospital for the foreseeable future, we decided to get our much too young child a phone. He wanted one in the worst way and had been dropping hints for weeks. I was avidly against this before our worlds were turned upside down but now we were hoping it would be his link to friends, classmates, and family while he was stuck in the hospital. Chris spent the morning calling store after store to find the red phone Vinny was requesting. Chris found one of the phones about thirty minutes away and left to get it as I stayed bedside. The pain meds were doing their job so Vinny was sleeping on and off throughout the day. The first thing he said when Chris returned, without opening his eyes, was "Did you get my phone, Dad?" With a laugh on our lips and tears in our eyes, Chris said, "Yes, it took four stores but I got just the one you wanted." This was one of the last times we heard Vinny's sweet little voice.

As time passed, Vinny's oxygen levels dropped lower and lower. The fluid in his belly was collecting and because he had been too weak to stand without losing consciousness, it started collecting in his lungs too. The nurses taped oxygen tubes to the side of his face so that he could breathe a little easier. His white blood cell count had skyrocketed from 80,000 to 175,000 by Sunday night, just forty-eight hours later. Because he was declining so fast, they scheduled him to be the first patient in line Monday morning for port surgery. The doctors chose to use a Broviac port which sits outside the skin with two ports attached so they can administer both the chemotherapy and other needed medications at the same time. A Broviac is not the standard treatment. It is the harsher of the two types of ports and is used when people may need more than one type of treatment at a time. They are placed into a vein near the heart so that drugs can enter the bloodstream immediately. He would start the treatments the next day, after it was safe to do so.

The nurses hooked him up to all kinds of machines to measure his vital signs. There was a certain threshold that his oxygen levels had to stay above. If they could no longer get him enough oxygen through the tube, he would have to be transferred to the Intensive Care Unit where they could give him forced air. Our main oncology doctor, Dr. Anca, assured us that unfortunately most every child with AML spends at least one stint in the ICU during their treatment.

We shouldn't worry and it was expected on some level because of the viciousness of the disease.

As the sun went down, I spent the next four hours watching the vitals monitor every fluctuation, every dip, as it slowly declined one number at a time. Beep, Beep, Beep, the sound slowly burrowed a hole into my brain. Occasionally, because of the meds, he would wake up and try to rip off the tubes. At one point, at about eight o'clock, when the room was dimly lit and somewhat calm, he ripped off his breathing tube, tripping the alarms and causing a cascade of even more intense, aggravated sirens. He was holding onto the breathing tubes so strongly that I had to get the nurses' help to put them back in place. I knew for those few seconds he wasn't getting enough oxygen. Internally I was screaming, "Breathe baby, you need that to breathe. Please keep it on. Please be getting enough air. This is the only way you can get the air you need."

After the nurses got him situated and resting again, I sat in silent anxiety, staring at that damned monitor until about eleven when a nurse came in and checked his vitals. She took a deep breath and calmly but wistfully said, "Don't be alarmed, but it's time. He's not getting sufficient oxygen for my comfort level and I am going to hit the red Rapid Response button. It will get very busy in here, with lots of people, very quickly. They will get him down to the ICU and get him hooked up to air that will be pushed into his lungs." And that's exactly what happened. As she hit the red button, the room went from quiet and dimly lit to bright fluorescent lights flooding in, red flashing lights and alarms sounding down the hall. Within minutes, a team of doctors and nurses rushed in to hook up oxygen tanks and get his vitals, each carrying their red emergency backpacks and preparing Vinny's bed to make the trip down to the Pediatric ICU. I tried to stay out of the way while I silently choked back mild hysteria.

If my anxiety was high before, it was off the charts now as adrenaline and fear entered the mix. As Chris and I were getting our things together quickly and making our way out of the room, I heard the team rattling off vitals, stats, and diagnoses. They mentioned that he had Acute Respiratory Distress Syndrome, or ARDS. ARDS is a serious condition that occurs in critically ill patients. It causes fluid to build up in the lungs and is life-threatening. Then I heard one of them say his appendix had likely already burst! (Did you hear that? YEP, I heard it too. Loud and clear. Not six days before, he was in an ER and a doctor felt his abdomen, without even removing the kid's shirt, and said he was just fine. Nothing amiss. He thought I was overreacting. Now it's presumed by all doctors involved that his appendix had likely already burst! Stomach bug my foot.)

CHAPTER 3

THE PICU

If you have never been in a Pediatric Intensive Care Unit, it is a different beast altogether. These are the sickest of the sick. Glass windows and doors are in a U-shaped formation so that every nurse can see into every room. Because the children are in need of more intense care, each nurse only has two patients at a time. The vitals for each room are on big black screens in the hallways so that they can be easily seen from any location and are monitored closely. The rooms are larger and more sterile because all treatments come directly to the patient. The patient never has to leave the room. Each room can be quickly turned into a surgical suite if the need arises. All equipment, x-rays, etc. are brought to them with the exception of the larger CT scan machine.

The other amazing thing about the PICU is that the doctors treat the body as a whole. They comb over every detail, every lab, x-ray, and scan and look at the whole picture instead of a different doctor for each specialty. They collaborate, research, and dissect each case collectively as a team. Our children's hospital is also a teaching hospital so there are many hands on deck. With teaching comes detailed explanations of each test and diagnosis at rounds every morning. Parents are encouraged to be present and questions are welcome.

When we arrived downstairs to the PICU on the second floor, I felt thankful. Thankful that he was getting the oxygen he needed. It was still only a tube coming from the wall, but the air was at a higher pressure. It pushed what he needed into his lungs without him having to breathe it in. I was thankful that there was one nurse who would be as keenly aware of his stats as I was because they only had one other patient. The realization that he was so sick that he needed this level of care was ignored and buried deep in my gut.

We settled into our room, with Vinny tucked in for the night, getting the oxygen he couldn't breathe in on his own. Our room was more spacious than the last with a larger bathroom and a side nook. The nook was at the back of the room with a single bed and reclining chair in front of a window that had a view of Charleston. The walls were blue and white, instead of the beige and cream on floor ten, which actually felt quite peaceful. Along the side wall across from Vinny's bed was a long, desk-height shelf that spanned the length of the room. Affixed to the wall was a flatscreen TV and next to that three floating shelves. It was a good room. I felt comfortable there with what we were about to face.

We only had to wait a few more hours until morning when Vinny could finally get his port put in. To see any sign of relief from the fever and the havoc being wrecked in his abdomen, we had to get the chemo started as soon as possible. The only way to kill the bad cells and get his body back on the path of healing was chemotherapy, and he couldn't wait any longer.

BEFORE

CHAPTER 4

A TALERICO HISTORY

Before I get ahead of myself, I'd like to tell you a little bit about who I am, who we are as a family, and my walk in faith.

I've been going to church for as long as I can remember. My parents were brought up Nazarene and Catholic and while they didn't attend church frequently as adults, they still had knowledge of Jesus. My mom would take us on Sundays until eventually my father decided to start coming as well. It took a little longer for him, but to this day he is still one of the strongest men of faith that I know. I grew up going to Sunday School and at the age of ten, my grandmother Nancy baptized me in front of friends and family. I learned about communion from her and how to keep Jesus in my heart. My parents loved each other and I grew up in a pretty happy and safe home.

I continued with youth groups throughout high school, attending countless conferences, lock-ins, and social events. Some of my closest, non-school friends were in that youth group and we spent lots of time together. On the flip side, I was also a normal high school girl, with common high school problems. I was in the marching band which kept my schedule very busy. We even got to go to California and perform at the Rose Bowl! I had a punk rock boyfriend with blue hair and went to a public high school with great friends and fun nights. Unlike some teens, we never got into TOO much trouble, but I may have flirted with the line a bit. Even at seventeen, I could feel the presence of the Holy Spirit. I had felt His peace, that goes beyond all understanding personally, and knew God heard my prayers.

A self-proclaimed artist since seventh grade, I followed my dreams to the American Academy of Art after high school. I commuted from the suburbs of Chicago to the corner of Michigan and Van Buren every day for four years and I loved every minute of it. At one point I was taking the max sixteen credit hours, plus I had two part time jobs AND an internship. I was going places and even though everyone said that being an artist wouldn't get me there,

I didn't let that slow me down. Being in the city was also one of my dreams. When I arrived at the top of the street from the Amtrak station each morning, I would take a deep breath and revel at the sights and sounds of Michigan Ave in downtown Chicago.

After I graduated college, I officially moved into the city I loved, got a great nine to five design job, and lived for myself. I still prayed, went to church occasionally, and I believed in God. But I wasn't following God's path, I was following my own. Being twenty-two and living in Lincoln Park with my girlfriends made for great fun, but not great choices. We worked during the day and partied at night. At that age it was "everything" to close out the bar at two o'clock in the morning and then pop up for work a few hours later with no problem. But when I would say my prayers during that time, I always felt like there was a glass ceiling above me and that my prayers were just bouncing off. I knew God was on the other side, but it was as if my prayers couldn't reach Him. It wasn't until much later in life that I realized it was my sin creating the separation from God. God was still there, I was just walking in the other direction.

Like many women in their twenties, I eventually became tired of the dating life and prayed every Sunday for

God to bring me "the one." I had endured my share of frogs and was desperately hoping to meet my prince and someone I could trust. Someone who had a similar background, similar interests, and a similar faith. And even though I was living for fun, He answered my prayers.

    I met my husband Chris on the shores of Lake Michigan one sunny day. It was June and the days were hot on the beaches of Chicago. We both lived in Lincoln Park at the time and it was customary after a late night of partying to spend the morning at the beach. I was there with my two roommates, my three next door roommates, and the three downstairs roommates. We all lived in the same building above the Clark Bar. Needless to say, we were a large group. I noticed a very good-looking guy sitting a few feet away from us. Most everyone in our group had gotten up and left for a walk while I sat by myself in a sea of crumpled beach towels. Very much NOT like my personality, I called out to him. I noticed he was alone, and I asked if he was at the beach by himself. He explained that he had just moved to Chicago and didn't know many people yet. He asked if I was there with a bunch of people. I sassily replied, "No, I just like a lot of towels." Apparently he found that amusing because he moved his towel to join our group! We chatted for a while until my friends returned and then took a walk down to the water. That's when I noticed the tattoo on his back. It was a large cross with the word Tetelestai across his shoulders. Tetelestai is a Greek word. My maiden name is Koulouris and my grandfather is Greek. We had always grown up with a little bit of "Greek" culture even though I am mostly Irish. Anyway, the Greek word caught my attention. Its meaning is "it is finished," which were the last words Jesus spoke on the cross. If his carved biceps didn't reel me in, this definitely did.

Chris is six and a half years my senior, a fact that I like to tease him about! Funny side note, his parents are six years apart, and his brother Jason and his wife at the time were also six years apart so it felt like another sign that he was the one for me! Chris grew up in a very similar home with strong Bible-believing parents who were supportive and caring of their two boys. Like mine, Chris's family saw the importance of traveling as a family, eating dinner together, and growing up in the church. Unlike myself, Chris pushed the boundaries of rules a lot further than I did. I always joke that he's lucky I met him when he was twenty-nine! I couldn't have handled his younger, wilder self. I have also always said that if the police bring one of our boys home in the middle of the night from mischief, he's the one answering the door as penance for what he put his parents through! To his credit, he's an extremely likable guy. He has a great family, great friends, and the guile to get out of trouble with natural charm.

We spent the rest of the summer together, having great fun in downtown Chicago. He had moved from Pittsburgh earlier that year to get his master's degree at Roosevelt University, but the program was finishing up and he would have to go back home at the end of the summer. Together we had decided that our paths were not to continue and at the end of the summer he would move home. That would be the end of our summer romance. We were both on the same page, until the night before his departure. All of a sudden, I felt this wave of fear and burst into tears telling him he couldn't leave. Now, I'm not typically the clingy type and any show of deep emotion leaves me very uncomfortable. I was just as surprised by the outburst as I think he was. But he had become one of my best friends. We had spent the whole summer together and suddenly the thought of him leaving for good was too much to bear. Truthfully, I think God was pointing me in his direction. Instead of running, Chris lovingly told me he felt the same way. We decided then and there to try a long-distance relationship.

It didn't last long, as neither of us wanted to move to the others' location, so we ended things after a few months.

That's when God stepped in. He started sending me little signs. First, I would see a Pittsburgh nightclub location we frequented in a Chicago newspaper. Then one night, at the Greek takeout place below my apartment, I was waiting on my order when this little three-year-old blonde boy stopped in front of me. He just stared at me! I waved and he waved back but he wouldn't budge. Finally, when his dad called his name to get his attention, it was the same name as Chris's only nephew at the time, who was also a blonde three-year-old boy. Now these coincidences might seem small to any other person, but if you have ever felt the Holy Spirit trying to get your attention it's crystal clear. It's like your vision zooms in and something becomes loud and focused. My heart started beating with the realization that this was something special, something to pay attention to. I will never forget the clarity of that little boy's bright blue eyes and light blonde hair as he stared at me and his father called his name. (There were NO other children in my life at the time! I was a twentysomething living it up in the city. Toddlers were NOT on my radar.)

And if *that* wasn't enough, my grandmother Nancy told me I was making a huge mistake. I told her that we had broken up and it wasn't meant to be and she said "No Kira, that is your future husband. I know it and you are going to marry him. You just watch." She was right, even though at the time I didn't believe her. Score one for grandmothers everywhere!

Chris and I still talked on the phone daily. We missed each other and so after some long conversations, I decided to move to Pittsburgh. Temporarily. To see if what we had was the real thing. The company I worked for gave me one year to work remotely with the intention of coming back to my position, in-house, when the year was up.

I worked from my tiny apartment in Pittsburgh for a year. I had always wanted to live on my own, give it the old college try. If Chris and I were going to possibly have a future, this was the time for me to do it. After the year ended, when it was time to return, Chris squashed those plans with a proposal!

We had traveled to Chicago for my brother's homecoming from the Army. He was on leave for a rare weekend home. We spent the night in celebration with my brother and his friends. The next morning, Chris wanted to take a drive before we went to the welcome home get-together the family was throwing for my brother. It was February and FREEZING in northern Illinois. Lake Michigan was frozen over to the point where there was bunched up thick sheets of ice frozen in place, battering the walking path. It was sleeting and a miserable bone-chilling cold.

Back when we lived in the city, Navy Pier would shoot off fireworks every Wednesday night during the summer. We spent many hot nights on that walking path looking over the lake with a bottle of wine, watching colorful fireworks while we were dating. Now, Chris pulled up to that very spot. We had to walk a bit from the car to get to the bike path, but it was SO SO COLD. I BEGGED him not to make us go out there. In fact, I put up such a fuss about not wanting to get out of the car and into the cold that he basically carried me piggyback-style to the lake's edge! The bitter wind was blowing so hard that my face hurt and I could barely see. As soon as we got there, I was like "Greeeat. Can we go now?" And when I turned around he was down on one knee, holding a box with a diamond ring inside. I said "YES!" and after hugs and tears he said "We can go back to the car now!!" I was ecstatic but maybe I did feel just a tiny bit bad for making it so hard for him to pull it off!

A year and a half later, my grandfather Leo married us at an outdoor gazebo in the suburbs of Chicago. The deal was that since we were living in Pittsburgh, the wedding and holidays would be spent in Chicago, and it was a GREAT wedding. Like every good wedding, some things don't go as planned, but none of those things could take away from the energy in the ballroom that night. Almost every guest stayed on the dance floor until the very last song. Chris and I had dubbed "I Gotta Feeling" by the Black Eyed Peas as "our song" and without requesting it, the DJ played it last. The whole crowd was on their feet with the energy of a downtown club screaming "tonight's gonna be a good night!" It was a wonderful wedding and that song has been an anthem for us for the last fifteen years.

In his early thirties, Chris didn't want to wait too long to have children. One year into our marriage he said, "It's soon, or never." So, we went with soon! But first we wanted to take one last trip together. Neither of us had ever gone on a mission trip and it was a bucket list item. So we got our malaria shots and hopped on a plane to Belize with the hopes of doing something good for someone else. We went with a Christian Missions company, with a well-planned itinerary, and met some wonderful people. The days were filled with caring for the local children at Vacation Bible School and evenings were spent in the church listening to amazing testimonies of God's forgiveness. One night, the pastor of a small American youth group that was also on our trip, asked if Chris and I would share our testimonies. In truth, we were a little scared and unsure. Neither of us had stories like the ones being shared of heartache, addictions, homelessness, and abuse. We were two white, middle-class kids from Christian homes getting ready to start a family. What inspiration could we give? In the end, we never got up on that stage. It didn't feel right at the time with so many who were suffering. Little did I know, my testimony was just a few years away.

In August 2011, we welcomed our first son Vinny. When Chris was a teenager, he had always envisioned his first son would be named either Vincent or Vincenzo. Since Vincenzo Talerico was a bit of a mouthful, we chose Vincent James after Chris's dad. Gosh this kid was amazing. As a tiny tot he always had a serious look on his face. It wasn't born of emotion but of trying to work out the function of the world around him. He was also fiercely independent. Many moms know what it's like to have a child attached at the hip, but Vinny was different. He wanted to do it all on his own and by golly he could! He was my easy baby, who slept through the night at four months, tried all the foods, and was speaking and running at lightning speed before he turned two.

Just shy of Vinny's second birthday, we welcomed my cuddly little blonde baby Chase. Chase had colic and cried every night from 5 p.m. to 11 p.m. for the longest first few months of his life. He didn't sleep through the night until eleven months, didn't walk until almost nineteen months, and did everything at the leisurely pace he preferred. He was also supremely stubborn when it came to the food he allowed in his mouth. As a toddler he would push his dinner plate to the middle of the table and calmly lay his head on his hands for the length of the rest of dinner as if to say, "I'm not eating that, and you can't make me." Lucky for him, he was so adorable in his stubbornness we did all we could not to laugh! That being said, he is the most compassionate, cuddly, loving child. He was unafraid to show us his affection and had the cutest little voice.

And so I was meant to be a boy mom. I could have gone for one more child, even though being pregnant wasn't my favorite thing. Chris felt that four was the perfect number for our family and with any more children we would be outnumbered. We knew in the future there was room for adoption and so together we settled in as a happy family of four.

Chris had always wanted to move South and for years we visited different towns, feeling out which would work for us. Charleston, South Carolina was the first place we visited that I fell in love with. Every other place we went, I would have made work for Chris. But Charleston called to me. A few weeks after Chase turned one, we packed everything up and moved from Pittsburgh to Charleston. God was so clear in this move. We had gone down a few weeks before to check out houses and out of the six houses we saw, I remembered the second house on the list as "the one." I had very few details about the actual house, only four pictures of it and even remembered the upstairs layout wrong! But still, I knew it was right. When we came home we decided to put our house on the market before we made an offer. It sold within the week and the South Carolina house was still available. Because it had already been on the market for thirty days, (which in Charleston means something must be wrong with it) we got a great deal. And there was in fact, NOTHING wrong with it! We truly felt God was opening doors in a very clear way. We started our life in the South and have cherished every day since.

CHAPTER 5

A TRIAL RUN

Because we were living in South Carolina, we spent many summers before school started in Pittsburgh visiting our Talerico family. Vinny would spend time out back with his Grams and she taught him about flowers and gardens. Because they lived in Pennsylvania, their backyard was a literal mountainside with waist-high railroad ties holding back the land. This was a perfect spot for little Vinny to sit and look closely at the potted marigolds that Grams planted every year. They would spend hours out there picking the seeds off the plants and learning how those seeds would become new flowers. He was always interested in learning new things even at a very young age.

My two little buddies couldn't have been more different. Where Vinny was riding dirt bikes, Chase was fascinated with computers. One time the boys had gotten kid quads, or four wheelers, for Christmas from Santa. Chris grew up riding quads in the hills of Pennsylvania and was thrilled to have two boys to pass that love on to.

That Christmas, just before we were about to entertain roughly fifteen people (most of our neighborhood was coming for Christmas dinner) the boys took them for a spin around the block with Chris. Vinny had the ability to feel the movement and speed and react as only a natural could. He could handle anything with an engine with the ease of his own two feet! Chase, on the other hand, gets his hesitation on such matters from me (sorry buddy) and as he took the corner around the block, he flipped the quad and it rolled right over him. He was only five years old and thank goodness he was wearing a helmet! Chris came in carrying Chase in his arms and his face was as pale as a ghost. After setting him on the couch, my mother and I ran over to make sure he was ok. We had been preparing the Christmas meal. The look on his face, and the look of his arm told me something was definitely not right. The moment we tried to touch his arm Chase started screaming.

That's when I decided we needed to go to the local ER. Chris scooped up our pale child and we got in the car to make the ten-minute drive. As I drove, Chase kept yelling, "Oww! Don't move Daddy please, it hurts!" with tears streaming down his face. I took every corner as slow as the car would allow but each bump was excruciating. At one point Chris said, "Kira, it's starting to bleed." When I looked back, we suddenly realized that what looked like a small quarter-sized circle of road rash was actually an open wound. Later they would tell us that it was a compound fracture of the elbow.

This would be my first experience with a broken bone and a child in immense pain. It is very hard to witness. When we got to the local ER they decided the best course of action was to brace the arm and take him in the ambulance, post pain meds, to the children's hospital where they could get a good look at his injury.

I climbed in the back of the ambulance on Christmas day with wonderful first responders who took us down to the Charleston Children's Hospital. After hours of x-rays and waiting they informed us of the compound fracture and said he would need surgery that very day. Because of the ghost staff, it wouldn't be done until around seven in the evening. While we were in the ER they showered Chase with Christmas gifts and did their best to make him comfortable. In addition to the anxiety and worry I felt, along with the fact that I was saving my calories for Christmas dinner and hadn't eaten a single thing before we jumped in the car, I was left starving and pining for graham crackers and apple juice!

At seven he got his surgery and my father drove up leftover Christmas dinner for us to enjoy in the waiting room. This was the only other thing I had eaten besides the crackers! As a testament to our friends and family, my mother continued to host a great Christmas at our home for all of our friends and family in an effort to make the day as happy for Vinny as he can remember, regardless of our Christmas absence. Our wonderful friends cleaned up our entire house so there was not a trace of the party we had missed. And though we were sad to have missed it, I was thankful to be surrounded by such a caring extended family.

Chase's surgery went smoothly and he came out with three pins and a cast from his fingers to his mid shoulder. He was admitted for the night and was so happy he even said, "Look mom! I can move my arm now!" as he waved his little green cast in the air. He eventually healed just fine, got the award for loudest screamer when they removed the pins, and since he was so young, only remembers a few details which I will never forget. As I look back, I consider this a trial run. One more step in a lifetime of stairs that would lead me to where I am today.

CHAPTER 6

I CAN DO HARD THINGS

Vinny took after his father in that he was great at managing mischief. He was curious about the world and the way things moved, worked, sounded, and felt. He sometimes got himself into a bit of trouble. I had to learn the hard way that boys get into trouble and that even in questionable circumstances, things would be just fine. We would always do what was best for our boys! Even the challenging times were innocent though. One time while Vinny was in first grade I got a call from his teacher. She was telling me how worried she was about our boy. She had placed him near a child who had some attention challenges and was hoping he would make a good role model for the other student. My first thought was, well I would NOT have made the same choice, but there you go. They got into trouble. They were caught rolling crayons into the adjacent bathroom.

Oh, my funny little boy. It was always about curiosity. Black sticky army men on the ceiling? How long would they stay up there? How high could he get them? My twenty-dollar bottle of purple shampoo? It was wiped all over the bottom of the shower and most of the bottle was down the drain. When I first saw this, I wondered why? But as I looked at its deep purple, almost glittery consistency, I thought, well I think it looks pretty cool myself so I can hardly blame him for experimenting with it! Of course, this was a thought I kept to myself. We can't have him dumping ALL of my expensive glittery shampoos down the drain!

As far as intelligence goes, my boys both have it in spades. They get this love for numbers, science, and the figuring out of life from their father of course. I, the painter/artist and avid reader of the family, wasn't much for math. We all have our strengths, right? I am so proud that they both got their brains from him. Beautiful, strong minds. Grades were never a struggle for either of my boys and they have always been at the top of their class. As a mom I never had to worry about either of them in this regard. Strong minds as far as stubbornness goes? Unfortunately, all four of us are blessed with that trait. Chris and I are both strong-willed but oddly we make a great pair.

We spent most of our time with our friends or "framily" as we like to call them. Vinny and Chases' two best friends were the children of our closest friends Faye and Justin, and so we spent most of our time together. Sarah was Vinny's age and Jake was Chase's. The four of them spent life together for the majority of what they can probably remember. In fact, Vinny LOVED Sarah. He looked at her as if she was his favorite person in the whole world. I don't mean it in a romantic kind of way, (even though we did joke that Faye and I could be in-laws some day!) but rather in a true lifelong friends sort of way. Faye and I were so similar that people often asked if we were sisters. Vinny and Sarah were similar too. The four kids did the neighborhood swim team together, and Vinny and Sarah both naturally excelled. They went to summer camps together and Vinny and Sarah were even in the same kindergarten class. They all rode the bus together and we often traded shifts with the kids at each house! Older at one house, younger at the other. It was a great time in our family life.

Occasionally, there are times in a normal day that it seems God calls to us. Sometimes we hear it, sometimes we feel it, and sometimes we miss it. In the months before

Vinny got sick I heard such callings, but it wouldn't be until we were in the hospital that I would recognize them for what they were. Divine.

Getting two boys to actually sleep at night was difficult. Vinny always loved when I scratched his back. After the umpteenth time of delaying his bedtime, he would finally ask if I could scratch his back while he laid down. At this point, Vinny was at the top of a very tall wooden bunk bed, so unless he scooted all the way to the very edge, I couldn't reach him. Just as I was about to say bedtime had already been delayed enough, I heard a small voice that said "Patience Kira, scratch his back." I am so thankful that I listened to that voice.

Another time, I was cleaning my bedroom and putting away laundry. I will never forget, my room was painted the color of butter, not my choice but I had not yet changed it since moving. Still, that color left my room feeling warm and sunny. Soft and comfortable. As I was folding the laundry next to my bed, with the sunlight streaming through the window and the sounds of an empty house when the kids are at school, I heard "I can do hard things." It literally stopped me. I'm not saying I heard it spoken out loud, but I thought it. Clearly. As I sat there thinking about that sentence, I said it a few more times in my head. Really chewed on it. I wasn't sure if I had heard it somewhere. Maybe in a song or something? Regardless, I decided I really liked it. I don't think of myself as a particularly strong person. Faith is really the only place I have ever considered myself strong. But at that moment I decided I wanted that statement to be true about me. Over the next few weeks, "I can do hard things," popped up in my head at frequent and random times. I thought about it and "chewed" on it every time it came.

It wasn't until I was standing in the ICU, next to my critically ill child, that the Holy Spirit whispered those five sweet words into my consciousness again. Suddenly I knew. With the clarity and realization that only the Holy Spirit can relay, those words had been from God. God was preparing me. He knew I was going to be standing in that room, facing the insurmountable, long before I even knew Vinny was sick. It was like a lightning bolt to my subconscious, and I knew God was with us. I was astonished that He had taken the time to prepare me mentally, in the months before, to stand by my child while he fought for his life. And fight, he definitely did.

CHAPTER 7

VINNY'S A ROCKSTAR

The progression of Vinny's disease was like something out of a movie. As we prepared for the Monday port surgery, we learned they would do a spinal tap and bone marrow biopsy at the same time. Since leukemia is a cancer of the blood, they needed to know what his bone marrow was producing to see if the cancer had reached his spinal cord and ultimately his brain.

"His brain?" I thought? "Please, God not his brain." The initial plan was to get the port placed on Monday March 29th and to start chemotherapy on Tuesday the 30th. Tests revealed that his oxygen, platelets, and hemoglobin were very low so they had prepared to transfuse his blood before the surgery if he needed it. Forty-eight hours after learning my son had cancer he was in the ICU on oxygen and getting a blood transfusion.

At 3 a.m. Monday, they ended up having to transfuse him. The results from his bone marrow biopsy revealed that 94 percent of the white blood cells his bone marrow was producing were cancerous. The team of oncologists decided that Tuesday was too far away and he would start chemo as soon as it was safe after the port was placed.

At 7:30 a.m., the surgeons came into the room to start the port surgery and we met the nurse that would soon become a fixture during our time at Shawn Jenkins Children's Hospital. Benjamin Woodhouse was a very tall, caring, dark haired, plant enthusiast who was also one of the head nurses in the PICU at the time. As he was prepping Vinny for surgery, he introduced himself as the one who would be caring for him after the port was placed and while he started his first rounds of chemo.

The time came for us to make ourselves scarce for a bit and we headed up to the window-lined cafeteria on the seventh floor. Chris and I were sitting at a corner table during breakfast discussing what was happening six floors below when Benjamin walked in. Seeing as how we had just met him, he came over to the table and assured us that Vinny was doing well and was in surgery. He was personable and energetic with respect to the gravity of the situation. I felt good knowing that such a caring nurse would be with us while we walked the PICU path.

Vinny came out of surgery and our doctors came to get us. They had one more piece of information we needed to know before we were allowed to see him. Because his lungs were so sick, they had to intubate him for the surgery. They would not be taking the intubation out while he was in the PICU until it was safe to breathe on his own. For that reason they would keep him mildly sedated until they were able to remove it. Coming back into that room with the flooding tears of relief that my baby had made it through his first surgery and then seeing him on a ventilator was heartbreaking. Anyone who came out of the Covid pandemic has a small understanding of what a ventilator is and how important yet terrifying it can be. Seeing that machine breathe for him was painful.

He was also hooked up to what I dubbed "The Christmas Tree." If you have ever seen those silver metal poles that administer medication through IV with the little beeping boxes on the front you will know what I mean. After the surgery, it had roughly seven beeping boxes and it looked to me like a Christmas tree of sorts. So that's what I started to call it.

While Vinny was in the PICU waiting for chemo to start, Dr. Paige and Dr. Anca came running into the room jumping up and down. The results from the spinal tap were in and even though the cancer was all throughout his body, it had not breached the spinal cord and his brain was clear and healthy! PRAISE GOD. This was finally a good piece of news that we needed to hear! It would not change the treatment process, but it wouldn't add the complication of treating his brain as well. If there was one thing we made sure to pray about, it was his mind. The thing that made him who he was. We prayed constantly for it to be spared from the disease.

That afternoon they started his first round of chemotherapy. The original intention was to start the next morning, but his cancer cell count was climbing so rapidly they made no delay and started it as soon as they were able. Then the oncology nurses walk in, wearing latex gloves and carrying a neon yellow bag with a caution sticker that said "DANGER" on it. Written across the top was "POISON." Because of the toxicity of chemotherapy, only oncology nurses could handle the medication. And they were pumping this glowing liquid into my baby. I don't describe it like this to say I disagreed with the treatment. It's more to understand the reality of how dangerous cancer is, that its only treatment is poison. The hope was that it would kill 100 percent of his white blood cells so that his bone marrow could start fresh with new, healthy cells. That was the way it was supposed to happen. If this didn't happen, we would start the process of a bone marrow transplant. I decided not to worry about THAT fresh hell until we happened upon it.

During the day there was a lot of help here, sit back there, wait for this x-ray, or that EKG, or some unknown blood indicator that I had never heard of until now. Because Vinny was going to be in the hospital for the foreseeable future, I decided to start a Facebook page. I had been updating friends and family as fast as I could but it had become more and more difficult. After what he had just gone through, I was so proud of my little fighter. I named the page "Vinny's a Rockstar." My initial reasoning was to keep anyone who wanted to know about his progress informed with the idea that later, when Vinny was off the ventilator and conscious, he could read all the support he was getting from the outside world. I kept it private but left it open to anyone who wanted to hear updates and pray for his specific needs. It started with friends and family and grew to over 700 people from all over the world, rooting for my little man. That Monday, my mother-in-law Georgeann posted that people in

Oregon, Washington, Illinois, Arizona, Florida, Ohio, South Carolina, Pennsylvania, and New Jersey were all praying for him. Having support from people we didn't even know was overwhelming and wonderfully comforting. God was moving and I was sure we were about to witness a miracle. What better way to spread God's word than for all of these people to see the miraculous healing of a very sick little boy.

The next day it was discovered that Vinny had "the common cold" virus and likely coupled with the cancer, that was what was causing his respiratory distress and lack of oxygen. The common cold is still contagious, and a droplet precaution was posted in yellow outside of his room. A tower station with yellow paper gowns, gloves, and masks was placed at the entrance of his room for everyone entering and exiting to keep the other patients safe. The hope was that he would only be on the ventilator for a few days while he was receiving his first round of chemo.

We also learned that the pain he had been feeling in his stomach ten days before was from an infarcted spleen. This was a word I had to look up after they said it a few times. It basically means "dead." His spleen was 90 percent dead by the time we'd reached the hospital. Are you kidding me? Not a stomachache, not a common virus, not his appendix, but the actual DEATH of his vital organ. I was also told that it is known to be a VERY painful thing to endure. Any number of tests could have found it if anyone had taken the time to look. In fact, if any one of those earlier doctors had ordered a simple blood test, the cancer would have shown up immediately. He could have been treated before he got dehydrated, before the cancer cells had time to multiply so quickly that he could no longer stand. Along with his spleen, his liver was also showing spots of infarction. The faster we could kill the cancer cells with chemotherapy, the faster they could stop his internal organs from dying. As much as I detested that neon yellow "poison" bag, I also knew he desperately needed it, and fast. His appendix had not yet burst, but it was extremely enlarged and inflamed. The plan was to leave it for now, but in the event they needed to, it would be removed later.

Instead of texting each family member who was waiting to hear updates, and because we weren't allowed any visitors in the hospital, I decided to post on the Facebook page as often as I needed to. New information was coming in hourly about his condition and it was a great way to ask for specific prayers.

This was my Rockstar post for the day:

WHERE WAS GOD?

March 30, 2021

Vinny is moderately sedated but not completely out. He can communicate in very small spurts. There are times when he is very uncomfortable with the breathing tube but he's tolerating it like A FREAKING ROCKSTAR. Pray for calm in his heart and mind so that he can endure this part of the trial. He's a super trooper. I'd be out of my freaking mind. I just keep taking comfort in the fact that hopefully he won't remember much of this part.

The issues have been pretty consistent from the start. We have already seen small victories and I have no doubt that God has a plan. We have a fabulous caring team sitting right outside our door, in a state-of-the-art intensive care unit. They can monitor his stats in real time from everywhere and they are quick to address needed adjustments. Please pray for them too as we are so thankful for their expertise and dedication to our kids.

Since Vinny had been sedated, albeit lightly, he was only able to respond to a few things by shaking his head or grabbing my hand. Eventually, in the midst of all the other therapies, they had a speech therapist come down. She created a custom chart for him with common words we used. Then he could point to the word on the chart to communicate. It is an amazing system they have worked out, but golly. I cannot imagine being in that situation from his end. He never once tried to pull the tubes out of his throat, which is common even for adults! Anticipating this, they strapped his hands to the bedside, but after a few days of realizing he wasn't going to fight it, they loosened his straps so that he could be more comfortable.

I decided to update the Facebook page daily as we started to get tons of comments, likes, questions, and prayers. We had almost a hundred comments a day and I quickly realized that there was a community of people invested in his well-being.

You know how people say that sometimes, in challenging circumstances, there can be a time where you get this superhuman energy or strength? That's what I was feeling. What's the next thing? What does he need today? How can I help? I never stopped. When I did stop, I waited. I coined the "coffee cup diet" by spooning leftovers anyone had brought, and many did, into the paper coffee cups that are free in the family lounge and throwing them into the microwave. I even thought, hey, maybe I'll lose a few pounds because I can't fit very much into a coffee cup! Those silly arbitrary thoughts in your head never stop.

When chemo starts doing its job there is a period where things get worse before they get better. It is a harsh but necessary medicine. At around 2 p.m., we got word that the chemo was working but his kidneys were no longer doing their job. He started retaining copious amounts of water and his torso, face, hands etc. started to swell. He was put on continuous dialysis and would stay in the PICU until his kidneys were able to function on their own and clean the toxins from his body. They wheeled in the big green machine with all of its dials and wheels. Dialysis is administered by surgically inserting large tubes into the vein of your neck to circulate and clean the blood in place of your kidneys. It could be days or weeks before his kidneys would start functioning again. Only time would tell. We got more good news when our oncologists informed us that his white blood cell count had gone from 175k to 86k in just one night! Thank you chemo!

That night we were pulled aside by Dr. Anca for "the big talk" as they refer to it. This is where you go into a small conference room and look at fifty plus sheets of paper with the side effects, risks, and cost of cancer treatments. And it is HORRIFYING. The side effects alone are enough to make a person nauseous but what choice did we have? He would die without it. When looking at the cost I couldn't help but ask, "Isn't this what bankrupts people?" It didn't matter, I would do absolutely everything I needed to do but every time I saw that Christmas tree I would add another dollar sign to the cost in my head. Dr. Anca said that bankruptcy could happen, but the cancer team did everything they could on behalf of their kiddos. They look at each of their patients as their own children and look after the families in that way as well. I took comfort in this as she explained that the largest bill they had ever seen sent to a family was 1.2 million dollars but they had an in-house legal team that would work with insurance companies on behalf of the families to make sure they were protected.

1.2 MILLION DOLLARS. I puked. In my mouth. Just a little.

Chris and I did pretty well for ourselves. He was in banking and I owned my own business. All of that was about to disappear. I would have to put my business on the shelf for a year, where it might not survive. All that I had worked for, gone with one blood test. Still, I was thankful. I was in a position to be able to put my business on the shelf and stay with Vinny full time. The majority of people in the world did not have that option. And their kids were in the hospital alone, all the time.

I was staying at the hospital full time now. My parents were still in town and staying with Chase, while Chris was going back and forth between the two. Things went up and down, good and bad, and the yo-yo roller coaster was exhausting. We went from having one nurse with two patients, to having a full-time dedicated nurse. After I saw those nurses leave, completely exhausted and still trying to catch up after a thirteen-hour shift from caring for Vinny alone, I began to worry. By the time he went on dialysis, he had two fully dedicated nurses all to himself.

On the 31st of March we were told he could come off of dialysis. His kidneys were doing great! The green machine was unhooked and things were looking up. By the afternoon he was put back on dialysis. The fluid retention was getting worse and our skinny little boy no longer looked like he normally did. I taped the pictures of him from the week before, at the pool with Sarah and Jake in Myrtle Beach, onto the glass door of his room. I wanted the men and women caring for him to see his true appearance.

At this point, I stopped taking pictures. I didn't want to remember this and I didn't want him to have to see it either. The cancer coupled with the chemo was wreaking havoc on his poor little body, but the cancer cells were down to 7,000 by the end of the third day! As I watched what was happening to him from my cream leather reclining chair in the corner, I started to have trouble concentrating. Usually an avid reader, I couldn't make sense of the symbols on the page. It was as if there was a disconnect from my eyes to my brain. I could no longer rely on a book to help me escape the hell I was living in. I also wasn't sleeping. I would take a quick nap when things were under control, from about 9 p.m. until 11:30 p.m. I would do a quick check-in to make sure everything was ok and then sleep again until 3:15 a.m. This seemed to be my waking time while I was there. The nurses would tell me that they had it all under control and I could go back to sleep, but I just wasn't capable of letting go.

If you don't have a 4 a.m. friend in times of trouble, you need to get one. My 4 a.m. sounding board was a mentor from a Bible study I was in a few years ago. Kathy would wake up around four to do her Bible reading each morning and would message me to check in. She always had a Bible verse or words of wisdom and I deeply cherished her messages. This was a difficult time of day, and to have a word from God was a breath of fresh air. Air to keep me breathing. The energy I needed to push on when the rest of the world was asleep.

Because of the dialysis, his temperature dropped from 104 degrees at the beginning of the week to 95.6 degrees, almost hypothermic. More alarms, more flashing lights. Another night of watching a monitor and every dip in a dangerous direction. They covered him with heating blankets and started warming his IV fluid to raise his temperature from the inside. Our wonderful friend Kimi made him a beautiful blue "Vinny's a Rockstar" embroidered blanket to keep him warm. As if worrying about his temperature wasn't enough, at 4 a.m. on April 1st, the dialysis machine went off, alerting anyone within fifty miles that something was wrong. After a minor panic attack the staff let me know that it was just a crimped cord and that I shouldn't worry about any alarms from that machine. "It is not a life-or-death machine and if it stops working, it won't hurt him at all," Benjamin informed me. I'm pretty sure I started growing gray hair that very night. It sure looked like a life-or-death machine with all of my baby's blood pumping through it.

On April 2nd, his blood pressure dropped and they had to administer epinephrine. Just a small amount, I was informed, and all this was to be expected based on the fight that was going on inside his body. Cancer, surgery, blood transfusion, respiratory distress, ventilator, dialysis, hypothermia, and now blood pressure. I posted to our hundreds of followers that his temperature rose two points and was in a good place for the first time in twelve days. I started posting specific prayers. I worried that they would be too graphic or sensitive for some, but I kept reminding myself that specific prayers get specific answers and the only people on the page were people who chose to follow along anyways. When I voiced my concern to the people following, I would get an overwhelming number of comments thanking us for the details of his health so that each could pray specifically. In truth, I had a lot of time just sitting in the chair between emergencies. Typing it all out, I think, helped my brain start to untangle the things I was seeing in some small way.

This was my post for April 2nd:

> On a whole he's looking up! They are even seeing signs that his airways are less inflamed. He continues to receive chemo and his white blood cell counts are under 1,000!!!!

SPECIFIC PRAYERS FOR TODAY

1. That the chemo wipes out all of the bad cells and his bone marrow eventually starts putting out normal white blood cells this first round. #remission #nobonemarrowtransplant

   (Remission after the first or second cycle is the goal but I'm saying why wait!!)

2. That the dialysis finishes taking away the copious amounts of fluid that have been wreaking all types of havoc in his body.

3. That the edema/cancer-caused pneumonia in his lungs, which already sounded much better today, completely clears, making it possible for him to breathe safely on his own.

4. That they are able to remove the dialysis port from his neck, and all of these other lifesaving wires and tubes BEFORE he

wakes up. I'm sure they will but this is a Mommy worry. I want some of these things gone safely so he barely even knows they were there.

5. That I get to hold my baby again soon. The only thing I've been able to do is put one hand on his forehead and the other on his poor swollen hand. I'm ready for a bear hug with my skinny little dude. In fact, I might make him finish his chemo sitting in my lap. Can you just see his embarrassment? I'll take a "mooooom" any day now!

Various people have told me how important these updates are for them. We have already seen what the power of so many praying does. "Where two or more are gathered, there too shall I be." I can't wait until I can post a picture of him with open clear healthy eyes. 🖤🖤🖤 #vinnystrong #vinnysarockstar #Godisgood

CHAPTER 8

CODE BLUE

During our time in the hospital, we received all kinds of mail for Vinny. Since no one was allowed in the hospital and no more than just family over the age of eighteen on the PICU floor, friends and family sent books, remote control cars, Lego sets, video games, and anything else a nine-year-old boy might enjoy when he's past this hurdle. I kept most of the packages unopened, especially the letters, in a safe place on the shelf so that when he was off the ventilator and battling his cancer back on the tenth floor, he would feel the love of his community. Kids LOVE personalized mail, and his shelf was overflowing. I couldn't wait for him to see it.

Vinny's class put together a gift card basket with all kinds of donated gift cards for him and our family. They even sent home his third-grade plant. Each student in the class had planted marigold seeds right before Vinny got sick. The same kind of flower he planted with his Grams. When he found out he'd be staying in the hospital he worried, "Who's gonna take care of my flower? I won't be able to take care of it while I'm here!" My mom Sherry said that while he was stuck in the hospital, she would water it and let it get plenty of sun so that he could see it bloom when he got home. Because you cannot have plants in the PICU or on the cancer floor, he would have to watch it grow from a distance.

Friday, April 2nd, was the day we were supposed to be leaving for our long-awaited family trip to Mexico. Nothing like that bitter realization to add to the grief of the day. Vinny's numbers were holding steady and I had finally seen a physical difference in his appearance, thanks to the dialysis. During the day, Vinny was kept comfortable but was able to communicate by blinking his mostly closed eyes or shaking his head slightly. He was able to pick which movies he wanted to listen to and I would read him the selections one by one so he could choose. When he was comfortable, I was able to run home and have dinner with Chase. Chase was disappointed that we weren't in Mexico so I brought home tacos. Needless to say, he wasn't impressed.

The next morning at rounds, we had a few new faces on the floor. We all gathered in the hallway, as we had every morning, to go over all of the tests and x-rays. He had been receiving them like clockwork every day for a while now and the process of examining all the facts was very helpful for me to hear. This time however there was a new young doctor presenting and when it came to examining Vinny's daily x-ray, he was shocked. This poor guy had not been on Vinny's case and was unaware of what he was facing. When he pulled up the scans he said, "Ok, so for today's x-rays his lungs look … wow, really bad, oh my goodness." The main doctor, whom we had been working with on the PICU on and off for weeks, jumped in and said, "Yes, but compared to yesterday there is improvement! Look mom, here is the comparison," as she directed me to the images. "We see improvement in these areas and he's doing better!" The look on that poor doctor's face was one of embarrassment and bewilderment. Hearing his new and outside perspective, even a student one at that, left me uneasy.

April 3, 2021

> Morning Update, are you all sick of me
> yet? We just had rounds which is amazing
> because all the team gets together and

goes over all the stats and numbers from the day. The attending does an exam every morning and then they address any changes. After that, the head doctor explains it all to us. They are so caring, compassionate, and willing to keep us educated and informed. I can't say enough about these wonderful people. Anyways, some of his issues are improving, others are still having trouble.

Prayer 1. Lord, fix his belly. Whatever is going on in there, not able to get rid of liquids, distension, pain, no bowel sounds, he had one piece of bacon last Saturday morning, knit it back together the way it should be. Help them find the issue and the correct way to fix it. He has had multiple CT scans, x-rays, and ultrasounds.

Prayer 2. Lungs. Prayers for clear healthy lungs. Pray today he gets rid of the wrong fluids to be able to breathe again on his own.

Prayer 3. Blood. Because the chemo is doing its job, his platelets are very low and he's getting transfusions. This is causing a petechial rash, very intensely, all over his body. There continues to be internal issues as well.

Prayer 4. Obviously FOR THE CANCER TO HIT THE PAVEMENT.

Prayer 5. He has more small waking moments where he is in pain or trying to tell us something. This is horrible for us but docs say it's great for his cognitive health. Pray for all that too. No pain, strong brain.

Sorry the post is so long. 🩶🩶🩶

    Seeing him unhappy was a challenge for me but I was honestly so proud that he had done so well for so long. I'd be in more than a bit of a bad mood if I was in his situation. Again, we hoped that he wasn't feeling any pain and that he wouldn't remember any of this but how could we know for sure?

Benjamin, Vinny's dedicated nurse, confided in us about the experience that led him on his path to health care. When he was fourteen years old he was climbing a large tree. He reached out for the next branch and accidently grabbed a high voltage power line that was hidden in the branches. In the millisecond it took him to lose consciousness, he realized what he had done and immediately thought, "Shit, I'm in trouble. This is it." A bolt of immense pain in the form of electricity rocketed through his body, sending him backwards through the tree. Thankfully a V in the branch below caught his ankle. His father scaled the tree the way only a hysterical parent can, and firefighters helped lower his lifeless body onto a gurney. As he came to, the firefighters were asking him where he felt pain. At the time, his right ankle was the main pain he was feeling. Everyone kept saying, "Are you sure it's your RIGHT leg that hurts and not your left?" He responded, "Why, what's wrong with my left leg!!??" He hadn't felt or seen it yet, but the electricity had exited his body through his left thigh, leaving a completely exposed wound that enveloped most of his thigh. He couldn't even feel it.

He spent weeks in recovery in the hospital after that and his mother was by his side the entire time. During one of our many side conversations, I asked him if taking care of

Vinny reminded him of being in the hospital himself. His response was, "No, but I see a lot of what my mother went through in you." These small connections, around Vinny's care, wove a tightly knit bond that none of us could have expected.

After hearing his story, I began to understand that he had firsthand knowledge that Vinny wasn't feeling any pain. He himself had spent medicated time in recovery and while he was there, he wasn't feeling pain or had any conscious recollection of the time he was under.

Signs that Vinny was awake or responding meant that his brain was functioning appropriately, even if it was hard for us to watch. I began to value these truly informational and completely meaningful talks with Benjamin.

Adding to my mounting concerns was that Vinny was starving. While he was sick that week before, he hadn't had very much to eat. I didn't push it because most moms know you starve a fever, and the kid didn't want food anyway. He had only eaten a single piece of bacon on day one in the hospital. Because of the distension in his belly, they tried feeding him via feeding tubes but there was too much pressure. Eventually they decided to feed him intravenously but that wasn't until after being in the PICU for a full week. I was told the cancer probably wouldn't let him eat anyways, even if he wasn't on a ventilator, a known side effect of cancer. As any mama knows, this would never sit right. Feeding your child is another basic function as a mom. Knowing that he had gone so long without food wove knots in my stomach even though I was told it was to be expected.

Easter came that Sunday morning and since I hadn't been home much, I went home early in the morning to be with Chase when he woke up. Chris had driven to the hospital to visit with Vinny while I was at home. We spent the morning together going through his Easter basket and swinging on the swings in our backyard, his favorite activity. We talked a bit about what Vinny was experiencing. He asked if Vinny was in pain and I explained to him how the medication works and how Vinny shouldn't be feeling anything. That he mostly slept, and when all of this is past us, he may not remember much of it. (This was my deep desperate plea anyway.) We discussed how Vinny wouldn't be home for a while and it would be months before he was home for good. Chase took all of this in stride with few questions and the general understanding that a seven-year-old child has.

At around two o'clock I headed back to the hospital to switch with Chris so he could spend Easter dinner at home with Chase and my parents. I was eager to get back. When I was away from Vinny's room, it felt as if I was not where

I was supposed to be. I had a constant feeling of anxiety whenever I was away. It wasn't until I stepped back into his room that I could breathe again.

> April 4th
>
> Well, the last half of today was not great. Prayers that we round the corner soon.
>
> We need more prayers tonight. He's having another ultrasound and a possible CT scan to see what the problem is in his belly. Pray that it is an easy fix.

That night they decided to take Vinny down for a CT scan. Because this was the only test they had to wheel him to, they decided the best way to do it was to bag him because there was a ventilator in the scan room and they would hook him up when they got down there. The nurses loaded up his bed with canisters of air and a portable monitor. They unhooked his ventilator and started to manually pump oxygen into his lungs while they traveled down to the first floor. They assured me they'd be back in no time and I should just wait in his room.

As Vinny was not able to breathe on his own, I was slightly anxious. I waited in the empty room, sat behind the curtain, and prayed. The wires and tubes were hanging from the ceiling unconnected and the light was warm and comforting because of the darkness just outside the window. As I sat there and prayed I heard two nurses talking as they walked by. They said, "Well, the two sickest patients are off the floor right now so we have a moment to breathe." This was the first time Vinny was off the floor. I knew they were referring to him. The other "sickest patient" was an eighteen-year-old girl who'd had a stroke and was left unresponsive. I had spoken to her mother in the family area a few days prior and my heart broke for her. "The sickest patient on the floor," I thought. In my heart I knew it was true. Most of the systems in his body were needing medical intervention. But the doctors and nurses assured me that they had seen it all before. Other children had similar experiences and were just fine. So I held onto their words. And we had hundreds of people praying every day for his healing. I knew God was going to do something amazing and I kept a firm focus on that.

All of a sudden, I heard yelling down the hallway. As his bed wheeled into view I could see a nurse straddling Vinny's chest yelling "CODE BLUE!" His pressure had dropped dangerously low because Vinny wasn't breathing. As nurses flooded the room, I was moved away from the bed so they could get him hooked up to the ventilator. As he had each time before, Vinny was fighting the manual pump. He wanted to do it on his own but the inflammation in his lungs prevented the air from entering. They got the ventilator into place and we all waited with baited breath as it started breathing for him again. As his stats slowly started to rise, we all took a sharp inhale. They took his vitals and told me he was picking up and getting the oxygen he needed. As I choked back a sob, I vowed to NEVER let them unhook the ventilator again until we knew that he was capable of breathing on his own. That night it took hours for his system to recover from the episode and the pressure of it all left him with two dark purple, swollen, bruised eyes.

CHAPTER 9

WHEN MARY WEPT

The next morning, April 5th, the results of the CT scan came back. His spleen was no longer viable. We discussed what it meant with the doctors. I learned that he would be on penicillin for the rest of his life but that he could live without his spleen just fine. The damage to his body was becoming permanent. The CT also showed that there were new spots on his liver and VOD (veno-occlusive disease) became the new concern. This is a side effect of chemo and its effect on the liver. They started getting his liver labs hourly to keep it under close scrutiny. The doctors said, "If we can get a week where he's JUST stable, that will be a win!"

April 5th

Let's focus on some Blessings today. Every day is hard in ways I never expected but I'm tired of typing those, so here are some YAY God's.

Yay God, his liver is holding even.

Yay God, his kidneys are paused but I'm firmly believing that's your doing.

Yay God, he recovered from last night a bit.

Yay God, no excessively bad news.

Yay God, day 8 of chemo. Almost done with his first round.

Yay God, our doctors and nurses are not only exceptional at what they do, they are compassionate, both to Vinny and myself.

Yay God. 🤍

On April 6th we did a public Call to Arms. A friend of mine had a dream the night before that we were supposed to get as many people together to pray over Vinny as we could, all at the same time. So we put out the call and at 4 p.m. Chris and I stood on either side of his bed and prayed. Around the world, churches, youth groups, small groups, and soccer teams all came together in prayer for my child. If that doesn't show the power of God, I don't know what does. "For where two or three are gathered together in my name, there I am with them." (Matthew 18:20)

During our time in between crises, Benjamin and I had many conversations about his life, our life, who Vinny was, and all kinds of medical things. I had been doing research online, never a good idea, but, as I said, I spent A LOT of time just sitting. I had seen an article about a person who had passed because of septic shock. Benjamin and I discussed at length about how it is a possible complication when it comes to so many things going into the body. He told me that it wasn't something I should worry about or research because septic shock is just a generic term that means infection. Vinny was already getting multiple antibiotics and there was no need to borrow trouble.

Wednesday, April 7

He seems to be holding steady!! He's off the blood pressure meds for now, they are able to keep going steadily with all of his machines! We'll take it!! Today is his last day of the first cycle of chemo and then he's got a few weeks of recovery before the next starts. Bad blood cells are down to 2 percent!!

He's even listening to our stories!

Special Prayers for today:

Liver, Kidneys, Lungs, Belly. God knows what he needs and pray that they are all restored to their natural born function.

Love to you all

Later that day I posted,

> I have been mostly focusing on prayers for major systems as those are the most

life-threatening. Those are still at the forefront but today we are starting to see smaller issues such as rashes, nausea, broken blood vessels, bruising, skin tears, and coughing fits, to name a few. Where he has been in pretty good spirits while sedated, you can tell today he does not feel well. He wears a pretty constant furrowed brow. He's trying his best to communicate with the ventilator but it's challenging. Today Speech Therapy, Occupational Therapy, and Physical Therapy all came at different times to try to assess and help.

Some prayers for physical comfort and internal peace would be appreciated. I imagine the days ahead will be challenging in all sorts of ways. I cannot wait until he is able to see all of the videos, letters, and packages he has from all of you. We are waiting until he is able to open his eyes and focus for longer than just a few seconds to let him open them. If you have sent something and I haven't commented, it's because it is still in its package. What nine year old doesn't like opening mail?! 🖤🖤🖤

Thursday April 8

I was about to post my daily update which was averaging 108 comments per post, when the nurse called me over to feel his arm. He had a large hard spot on the back of his arm the size of a softball. Benjamin was standing at the end of the bed with me and the other nurses on each side. I looked up at Benjamin and said, "Isn't that a sign of a blood clot?" He shook his head and lovingly said, "Man, I hate it when they are smart." He was hoping he could have spared me that one worry but in fact I knew the indications and concern before they even said anything. They called for an ultrasound. He had been having x-rays every single morning to monitor his lungs, EKGs to keep an eye on his heart, hourly labs to watch his liver, and now an ultrasound to check his veins. Thankfully we eventually found it was just a large hematoma from his numerous IVs. No blood clot in sight. No big deal, just a softball-sized internal bleed in his arm. Can the kid get a break? Sheesh!

That evening Vinny was holding strong. Everything was in a wait-and-see state, stable as can be and I hadn't been home much. Benjamin and Chris said we were in a good spot for me to go home and get a good night's sleep. Benjamin was off for the weekend and introduced us to the nurses that would be on duty. Since even leaving his room gave me terrible anxiety, I doubted that I'd get any sleep but I needed to go home and see Chase. My parents were still holding down the fort for us, even though they were supposed to be packing up their home in Florida. We had dinner, and I hung out with Chase a bit.

At about 10 p.m. I got a call from Chris. There were new doctors for the night, doctors we hadn't met before and something intense was happening. Vinny's blood pressure was dropping fast and was dangerously low. They wanted to take him downstairs for a CT scan. I SCREAMED into the phone that they would do no such thing, that he wouldn't survive it, he'd barely survived the last one. He was too weak and was in even worse condition now than the last time.

Chris got off the phone and the doctors conferred about what to do. Vinny's heart could no longer take the stress of what was happening to his body and was quickly giving out.

When they called me back, it was the doctor this time. He sternly said, "Listen. I am afraid Vinny is not going to make it through the night. His system is failing, and we have to put him on bypass. The surgery for bypass or ECMO is very severe and he may not even make it through the surgery. We will have to place an even larger tube in his neck and another large IV in his thigh. There are many complications with ECMO but if we don't do it he won't make it until morning." We realized there was no choice and made the call. I was frantic. Chris asked my Dad to drive me to the hospital because he was afraid I'd be too distracted to safely drive the thirty minutes downtown.

My dad and I drove in silence. Inside my head thoughts were going a million miles a minute and I prayed that my little boy would make it through the night. The highway was empty as we raced across town in his gold van. My Dad parked and we RAN through the hospital. I didn't even stop to show my badge. I just ran right past security screaming that it was an emergency and I was headed to the PICU. My dad stopped at the guard station to check in and then continued onto the second floor. Even though he wasn't on the list they allowed him to come in at this dire time. I made it to the room first and asked the nurses to watch for my father. The PICU doors lock as they shut and without a badge, there is no entry.

The hospital was quiet. All of the important lights were on, but it was calm and there were very few people in the hallway. Exactly the opposite of what was going on inside me. I made it to the room just as they were saying we only had a minute to say goodbye.

They had transformed the room into a surgical suite. Outside sat technicians and machines and carts with tools I had never seen and hope to never see again. There were people everywhere. New doctors, head surgeons, oncologists, neurologists galore. They were spinning the bed so that it sat longways in the center of the room instead of against the wall to make room for techs to work on all sides. His bed lifted up to chest height as they started hooking up even more monitors and medications. They turned on this ethereal bright white light that I hadn't even noticed before in the center of the ceiling. Chris grabbed Vinny's left hand and I grabbed his right. Chris and I told Vinny that we loved him and that he'd be ok and we'd be right outside the door. Thoughtfully the doctors said, "we have to start now, there's no more time."

A nurse whisked us out of the room and into the dimly lit hall where we met my father. The nurse turned to us and said, "would you like me to call the chaplain now?" I was so shocked by the question that I just looked at Chris and my father. Chris looked at my dad and said, "No thank you, we have everything we need." I was so glad he answered because I had no idea what to say. Up until this point, I never really pondered the idea that Vinny wouldn't make it. She ushered us into the room that ran along a wall perpendicular to Vinny's. Also with glass doors, you could see things coming and going out of Vinny's room, but not inside it. The adjacent room was empty and dark. Only the nightlight above the bed was lit. Compared to the sense of urgency that was happening in the room just across the hall, this one was still, cool, and quiet. There were no sheets on the vinyl bed, no chair. The only seating was a padded bench at the back of the room.

One of the head surgeons came in to chat with us about what was happening. Because of the swelling in Vinny's abdomen, there was too much pressure for the ECMO system to work. The only way to relieve the pressure was to make more room, which meant cutting an eight-inch incision down his torso. This was the only way to save his life. What choice did we have? It was all moving at warp speed and we were clueless as to what ECMO even was. Before leaving she asked again if we were ready to see the chaplain. All in all, we were asked three times if we wanted to see the chaplain and each time Chris said, "No." After our consent she left the room to begin the procedure.

The nurse wheeled in a chair but I opted for the floor. In fact, I was left with such a sense that my child wouldn't make it through that surgery that I sat with my back to the window. I thought for sure I was going to see them slowly walk out of his room, like some sort of drama, head shaking low and pulling off rubber gloves, and I would know he was gone before I even heard the news. I couldn't bear to witness that scene so I sat with my back facing the door. My dad sat on the padded bench and started to pray silently. Chris sat down beside me and we started to pray as well, huddled together on the floor.

We sat on that hard floor in that very cold room for what felt like hours. Chris got out his phone to turn on a Christian song someone had sent him. It was "The Blessing Song" by Kari Jobe and Elevation Worship. But the one that was sent to him was a Pittsburgh rendition. At that time people were recording solo songs and splicing individual artists together to create a whole orchestra from all different locations. Coronavirus was still an issue and in this version each line was sung by a different Christian church in Pittsburgh. As we sat on the floor, we watched the video and listened to the music fill the room from the tiny phone speaker.

> *The Lord bless you and keep you, Make His*
> *face shine upon you and be gracious to you*
>
> *The Lord turn His face toward*
> *you and give you peace*
>
> *Amen, amen, amen*
>
> *May His favor be upon you and*
> *a thousand generations*
>
> *And your family and your children, and*
> *their children, and their children*
>
> *May His presence go before you, and*
> *behind you, and beside you*
>
> *All around you, and within you*
> *He is with you, He is with you*

*In the morning, in the evening, in
your coming, and your going*

*In your weeping, and rejoicing
He is for you, He is for you*

*He is for you, He is for you, He
is for you, He is for you*

He is for you, He is for you (I know, I know)

Amen, amen, amen

    When the song finished I sat there crying and turned to lean on my husband. He was sitting on my side, facing the bed. I twisted my torso and I threw my arms over his shoulders, stretched out in an awkward position and wept. That's when I saw it.

    As I stared over his shoulder, up in the corner of the ceiling, in that dimly lit blue room, I saw the eyes of Jesus looking back at me. Not just his eyes but his whole face as if he was hung on the cross, head hanging down and to the side. His deep dark brown eyes were staring at me with intent. I could see the dark strands of thick black hair and the crown of thorns around his head. He had a dark beard and a medium but dirty complexion. His arm, which was nailed to the cross, was extended in my direction as if his fingers were reaching out to me.

In that moment, as I stared in wonder back into those dark, ominous eyes, I heard myself weeping and thought, "I wonder if this is what Mary sounded like." It was such a quick thought, spoken as if by me, but not at the same time. I had the thought at the same moment I saw Jesus's face and outstretched hand. And then, it was as if I could see myself turned, legs stretched out behind me, sitting under the cross as Mary has been depicted in so many paintings. Reaching out to her beloved son and weeping for him. I was in that exact same position, staring up at her son on the cross. My next thought was, "Well this is a really strange thing to be thinking right now!" What was happening? It was all so clear. I focused my eyes and noticed that I could still clearly see the corner of the ceiling, but I could also see Jesus's face and outstretched hand in front of me. It felt calm. There was no fear, only peace. But his presence was somber. It didn't feel happy or sad or scary, but almost foreboding. It was cool, and dark. All was still, including the image of Jesus. He never moved or said a word, but his eyes were piercing. They called to me.

At that moment the only thing that I could think of was that Jesus was reaching down for Vinny. I thought maybe he was reaching down to bring my child home to Heaven and soon we would get word that Vinny hadn't survived the surgery. I wondered and waited for that revelation as the vision disappeared. I considered that maybe Jesus was showing me so I could know that when he died, it was God's will. I had seen it in person, and I would know it was ok. That was my best interpretation of what I had seen at the time.

I sat up from my leaned over position and said quietly, "Well that was weird. I swear I just saw Jesus." But neither Chris or my dad heard me. I kept the vision close to my heart, unsure of what to make of what I had just seen, hoping that my understanding was wrong.

Shortly after, the doctors came in. Shockingly, the surgery had gone well. The ECMO was pumping and Vinny was as stable as someone on life support could be.

Again I saw Jesus's eyes, burned into my thoughts. What could it all mean? The doctor had explained that he had an eight-inch incision on his belly. There was a wound vacuum holding the incision open for a time, and it would slowly close over the next few days, little by little, as his body allowed the pressure to dissipate. Also, during the procedure they had, in fact, removed his appendix.

There was still no indication as to what caused the emergency situation in which his heart rate plummeted. The best answer was that there had to be an infection somewhere in his body, better and more commonly known as the dreaded sepsis. That's right, sepsis. The article and my conversation with Benjamin came right back to me. This couldn't be happening.

His Christmas tree grew as they added more antibiotics, medications, and literally the kitchen sink. He now had three separate Christmas trees, each holding every sort of medication, hoping to quell the mysterious infection hiding somewhere in his body. We would be allowed back in the room as soon as all of the surgical equipment had been removed. A short while later the staff brought us in. The change in the room, and what we had been previously living in, was drastic.

CHAPTER 10

PAUL, MARY, AND MARTHA

As we entered the room, the urgency that could be felt in the air before was replaced with a steady pace of monitoring, cleaning up, and putting the room back to a tidy position. Vinny's bed now lay in the center of the room with what I can only describe as a locomotive engine at the head of his bed. Now this is an exaggeration, but the ECMO, or Extracorporeal Membrane Oxygenation Machine, was about as tall as I am, as wide as the bed itself, and had pipes and wires and dials that looked like a water meter, all moving with a quiet hum. The ECMO machine is a life support system that pumps and oxygenates the patient's blood, allowing their heart and lungs to rest and heal. This is what

Vinny needed. It was buying him time. His heart and lungs were too weak and sick to continue on their own. This machine would do the work for him so his organs could regain their ability to function again.

It had its own computer to monitor the progress, and large tubes, even bigger than the dialysis tubes that led straight into Vinny's neck. Because of the danger of blood clots and severity of the ECMO system, he was placed on a paralytic and stronger medications to keep him completely sedated and immobile. His body temperature was being controlled by the system as well so there was no need for blankets to keep him warm. Something about this detail scratched at the mama bear deep inside my chest. All I wanted to do was cover him up, keep him as warm and as comfortable as possible. But we were past that point now.

Because I was unsure what the ECMO system even did, I made the mistake of googling its meaning. After the definition, the first question on Google is "What is the survival rate for ECMO?" The answer was 25 percent. I immediately slammed my computer shut and tried my best not to lose my lunch. Then I reminded myself that God was in control of this situation, not Google. And God didn't follow statistics.

Friday, April 9

The reason I am sharing all this is because even on his deathbed Jesus had a plan. If I don't share the journey, then you all can't be witness to the greatness of God. Praise God, last night was not his night to leave us. Although, his timeline at this point is unclear. They told us if he wasn't put on bypass, he wouldn't make it through the night and if he was put on he might not survive. He made it through the surgery and now every department in the hospital is trying to figure out what happened. They are unclear as to why things changed so quickly. The only thing they can think of is an infection and are doing their best to fight it with every available medicine. They are still working hard to comb over every possible issue and we will reconvene at one with the heads of all involved departments. He is having x-rays and ultrasounds and EKGs galore.

Something had changed in me since the night before. I could still see Jesus's eyes so clearly in my mind but I had so many questions. Why that vision? Why that position? Why the comparison to Mary, the Mother of Jesus? What was the meaning? If God had not taken him home, I didn't understand what he was trying to tell me.

That all-consuming adrenaline that had been coursing through my system for the past fifteen days was wiped out. In its place, I felt unrest. I've read that in the face of trauma the amygdala center of the brain responds with either fight or flight. Mine had chosen to fight fiercely. From one emergency to the next I was ready to go without sleep, without the need to catch my breath. I had that superhuman energy that allows you to continue when normally you may have needed to rest. But after that night, I was no longer full steam ahead. The confidence I had in his ability to recover was starting to waver.

The toll that all of these medications and procedures were taking on my son's physical body was almost too much for a mother to bear. His kidney output was so bad at this point that his urine bag was almost black. His skin had suffered rashes, tears, and now because it had been a while without moving he was developing large blisters. Hematomas, black eyes, swelling, and now two very thick tubes came out from his neck. He had four IVs in different spots and of course his double chemo port. And let's not leave out the eight-inch wound vac on his stomach. It was all becoming too much. How much torture can my baby take? I spoke with the nurses about keeping his stomach incision covered. I had seen enough in the past two weeks and I didn't want this image seared into my memory. Soon enough, we'd be on the other side of this horrible nightmare and I would leave all this behind us. They had it under control. There was nothing I could do to change or help the situation, so I didn't want to see it. They kept a loose blanket over his midsection for my sake.

One of the main side effects of ECMO is uncontrolled bleeding. Because the system does the work of your heart and lungs it takes large amounts of Heparin, a common blood thinner, to move the blood smoothly through the tubes. A dedicated nurse monitors only that machine, checking the tubes repeatedly for clots because it can be a common and dangerous problem, and/ or the leading cause of death by ECMO. Because of the Heparin, he started bleeding. He slowly bled out of every IV port, around his ECMO cannulas, and even his mouth filled up with blood. When I saw this, I crumpled into the chair with tears in my eyes. Chris ran to get the nurse. They suctioned his mouth and placed gauze in the necessary places. I was about to file this in with the wound vac into the "no person should have to ever experience this and no mother should ever witness her child going through this," category in my brain. That file was soon to be purged as soon as he was off this dreaded machine.

I was assured that all of this was manageable and normal and as long as the bleeding stayed out of his brain, he would do just fine. An intracranial hematoma or brain bleed was the most severe of the side effects from the ECMO system and was often the cause of the low survival rate as well. The way they monitored this side effect was to check the size of his pupils every few hours or so. If they were even, everything was fine. But if one or both pupils were blown, meaning one larger than the other, that could mean a bleed in his brain. To this point God had protected his brain, and as long as his brain was still the intelligent, funny, happy Vinny we knew, we would continue to try desperately to keep up with his physical needs.

But that didn't mean it didn't affect me deeply. I felt deep shame in the realization that it was hard to look at my baby. I didn't want to remember seeing him this way. It is hard enough to witness all that I had seen already and this was too much. I kept reminding myself that when this is all over I would have plenty of time to see him the way God made him, not the way this disease had changed him. So I focused on his feet. This is a memory that brings pain and shame and a feeling of cowardice. It was the only part of him that still looked just like my baby, feet that looked like his daddy's. But as a mom it was devastating. I began having trouble eating. I spent the morning curled up on the cot crying. When I stood over him all I could think about was that this MOUNTAIN of issues he physically had to overcome was extensive and possibly insurmountable. I wasn't completely sure now that he could do it. In place of blind optimism and assurance was dread.

My wonderful husband could see the change in me. He thought to surprise me with a favorite lunch of mine, French food, and walked blocks to get it. We had gone to Paris on our honeymoon and trying foods from all of our travels was a thing we did together. This included a Croquette Monsieur sandwich. I hadn't heard of it until we got back from our honeymoon and was so disappointed I hadn't known to try it there! Ever since then, it has been a thing we enjoy. It was the sweetest gesture he could show me and I will never forget the gratitude I felt for such a kind thought for me, when he was struggling with the same reality. I slowly lifted the sandwich to my mouth. I could barely force my mouth to open. I made myself take a bite because he had gone through such lengths to do this beautiful thing for me but all that came were tears. It was like the act of eating was excruciatingly painful to my soul. There is no other way to describe it. I just couldn't. I choked down as many small bites as I could muster out of love for my husband. Deep down I thought, this isn't good. Those who know me know my love for food. We continued to sit a somber vigil at his bedside for the rest of the afternoon.

Doctor Paige came to speak with us and addressed the situation. She told us she knew this was hard and seemed impossible. She told us about another little boy, who had been in the exact same position, with the same prognosis and disease on ECMO just last year and now he was running through the hallways upstairs just like every little boy should be. She told us that he could get through this, and we just had to give his body time to heal from the vigorous chemo treatments, the leukemia, and the distress his body had endured. The first forty-eight hours were key. If we would hold steady for a few days he would be able to pull through. Now it was a waiting game.

During the course of our conversations with our many nurses, Chris came across a wonderful piece of information that gave us some hope. During the night, while I was looking into Jesus's eyes in the other room, the three nurses that were dedicated to pulling Vinny through the surgery were named Paul, Mary, and Martha.

If you have background knowledge of Bible history, you might recognize those names as some of the most famous. Paul was originally named Saul, a Jewish man that was one of the most notorious Christian persecutors in the time after Jesus. He tracked down and stoned many followers of Jesus Christ. A resurrected Jesus met him on the road to Damascus and confronted him. Saul was blinded for three days because of seeing the Messiah himself. He went on to preach the gospel to people all over the continent and became one of the most prolific writers of the New Testament. In fact, he is attributed to writing twelve to thirteen books in the New Testament. He wasn't even one of the first twelve apostles but because of his legacy to the faith, he is often considered one of the most well-known apostles of Jesus Christ. He was a man that suffered immensely, saw Jesus's face, and went on to deliver the good news of Jesus's sacrifice.

I gather that most people know who Mary is but just in case, she is the mother of Jesus. The one who birthed him, raised him as her own, and wept under the cross when he died. But there are quite a few important Marys from

Jesus's time, including Mary Magdalene and the story from Luke about the sisters Mary and Martha. When Jesus came to their home, Martha did all the things that we women do when important company is over, trying to make everything perfect. Her sister Mary sat and listened to Jesus speak. Martha became indignant that she was doing all the work when Mary wasn't helping, but Jesus said, "Martha, Martha, you are worried and upset about many things, but only one thing is needed. Mary has chosen what is better, and it will not be taken away from her." The moral of their story is that if Jesus is in your presence, will you focus on all the things around you? Or will you be still and focus solely on him? And while hospitality is important, it can become a distraction. Just like many good things in our lives can distract us from what is really important. The "doing" of the things can take us away from being present in most situations. Ultimately for me it was being present in that moment and focusing on Jesus and setting the rest down at his feet.

Paul, Mary, and Martha had cared for Vinny that night. Of all the names of all the nurses in the hospital, those were the three that were helping my son at the exact same time we were calling on Jesus for a miracle. So "Where Was God" at that point? I have no doubt he was in that room with

Vinny and his wonderful nurses, even as He showed me His face.

That weekend we hit our number of days needed to add two more people to the visitor list. For the first time my parents were able to come visit us and see Vinny in the PICU. I was so relieved to have my parents with us even if only for a short visit. Because of Covid, it was just us three. No one else knew what was really happening besides my Dad and my neighbor Claudia. She was a nurse at the neighboring hospital and was able to check in on us one time. None of our close friends, neighbors, or family had seen him since he was admitted.

There were these two worlds, one outside that was mostly nonexistent to me, and the one inside, that only Chris and I knew about. Really knew. Having my mom and dad by our side was a welcomed strength. And do you know what she said? "He looks great! Really! Aww buddy." She was so optimistic. The one thing, the most important thing I had lost, she was able to provide. That blind optimism that everything was gonna be ok. That it's not as bad as it seems and that he looked good! This was the first outside perspective I had and it shocked me in such a wonderful way. She wasn't looking at him through the eyes of what I had seen, every skin tear, every x-ray, every cascading disaster. Of course, she knew about all of it, but this was the first time she had seen her grandson in over two weeks and she looked at him with eyes only a grandmother could. She brought me hope.

Friday update.

After some hard conversations we are just playing the waiting game. Chris and I are staying in the hospital and Mom and Dad were able to come see Vinny. They said the first 24-48 hours are critical so pray that his heart holds on until he heals. For now, we just wait and pray. If God is to work his healing power, we're about as far down the line as we can get. Thank you to the hundreds of people who are praying for him around the clock. We are so thankful for your prayers and support. Until tomorrow.

Saturday Morning Update.

24 hours, God is Good. He's holding on. There are so many details of every

system in his body and so many levels and complications and small gains it's just still a wait and see. They are doing all the things. Let's focus on the good because there's too much scary to share.

Good. He's tolerating ECMO. His lactate level, something we've learned a lot about, is a tad lower. His liver levels are mostly doing good. Our doctors and nurses are beyond talented, amazing, and compassionate. God is Good, your prayers are being heard. And if teeny tiny baby steps is what it's gonna take, then we'll take them with Him.

Vinny will be having three procedures from now until noon tomorrow. Specific prayers, and I'm sorry, I know it's hard, but I ask for prayers in controlling the bleeding. It's common for patients on ECMO and it's a risk. So Dear Lord please work against science to stop excess bleeding during the procedures and honestly from here on out. This is one of the parts that has been specifically hard for me and I am so sorry and trying not to be graphic. So all prayers are appreciated. God has answered many so far. With love and gratefulness.

In true Vinny fashion, he was fighting the ECMO machine. His independence and stubbornness to do things on his own was showing even when he was virtually in a medical coma. He was on the child-sized machine but it wasn't working as thoroughly as he needed and during the night they had added an extra pump to clean the blood. Over time though, they decided he would need to be put on the adult machine. My son has been a fighter this whole time. In fact, his whole life! He's an independent and problem-solving kind of little guy. And this was just another example of how he would give everyone a little grief. And honestly it brought a smile to our faces.

Procedure #1 Finished. They had to change him from a child ECMO machine to an adult one. They thought the child one, numbers-wise, would be fine but said Vinny wasn't playing by the rules. We laughed. That's our Vinny!! He transitioned fine and we ask for prayers that this circulation is what we need for a more complete healing and turnaround.

As if ALL that was happening wasn't enough, we had another minor (in comparison but not reality) complication. Because he was sedentary for so long, drop foot had started to occur. Foot drop is when the top part of your foot no longer holds itself up. When you lay down with your heel to the floor, your toes should point to the ceiling. But when you start to have underlying neurological, muscular, or anatomical problems, the center of your foot will start to bend so that your toes are lowered and eventually face forward instead of up to the sky. To avoid this, physical therapists have all kinds of different solutions. One of these solutions being he wears a boot for a few hours a day. This holds his foot in a flat shape because he was already showing signs of weakening in his feet. After a few hours, when they came to remove the boot, the end of his foot and toes were completely white and the pulse in his foot was weak. The circulation to his toes had been restricted because of the boot combined with the ECMO system pumping his blood. Enter Mom panic mode. This kid has gone through so much already the LAST thing he needs is to wake up with his foot amputated! So I stood there. By his bedside. For two straight hours massaging his calf and foot, being careful not to hurt his delicate, blistering skin, WILLING the blood to make it to the end of his toes. With every stroke I prayed for God to save his foot. By the end of the night the color had returned, and I collapsed into my chair with a whimpering sigh of relief. It was another small answered prayer. And yet a huge, huge win.

It was coming close to the time my parents would be moving to Charleston. In fact, it was Saturday and their entire Bible Study group was coming Monday to help pack up their Florida home. They were supposed to have had these past two weeks to get everything packed up but since they were here helping us, nothing was done. This left them with a whole house to pack up in a very short time. We discussed Vinny's situation and decided if he was still holding steady on Sunday they would return home to Florida, pack up and finalize the closing on their house, and then return at the end of the week as previously planned.

> *The LORD knows all human plans; he knows that they are futile. (Psalms 94:11)*

Knowing ahead of time that my parents had to head home to pack up the house, Chris's parents had arrived in town from Pittsburgh. I was so thankful that Chase had a house full of grandparents for these hard weeks when his parents couldn't be there with him. They had not yet seen Vinny and they were next on the list to visit.

Sunday Morning

Praise #1. Last night there was some worry about blood reaching the end of his foot. This morning most of the color and pulse has strengthened. THANK YOU LORD, like he didn't have enough on his plate!!!!

This morning starting at eight he will have another surgery on his belly that will last roughly two hours and then a procedure on his lungs right after. GOD we pray for great results that will move us towards recovery and all good news. We pray that during these surgeries your hand stops any bleeding.

The next two procedures would be done together on Sunday morning. They wanted to try to slowly close his stomach wound a little bit every few days. Additionally, the x-rays he had been having on his lungs every morning showed that after his episode, his lungs had gone completely white. Our small wins and improvements over the last few weeks were gone and his lungs were so infected they decided while he was under, he would have a surgery to clear out some of the infection and a biopsy to see what it was that was causing the drastic decline. It was a full in-room surgery for both procedures, so we would have to leave for a few hours.

The doctors suggested it would be good for us to actually leave the hospital during his three-hour stint. I wasn't happy about it but Chris suggested we take a walk outside. It was an absolutely beautiful Southern day. Warm sunshine, a cool breeze, and not a cloud in the bright blue sky. The children's hospital is a few blocks from the heart of Charleston so we decided to walk to King Street for breakfast. Virginia's on King was close to the street we were at so we ended up there. We quickly sat at a little table towards the front, in the center of the restaurant. A lovely woman named Octavia was our waitress for the morning. She was pleasant and bright. Chris ordered breakfast and I ordered the crab soup, a well-known dish in the lowcountry. Any kind of soup is my go-to meal, any time of the year, any flavor, I love soup. But I was struggling something fierce. As I had mentioned before, leaving the hospital in any capacity gave me an abundance of anxiety. Knowing that he was having surgery as we sat there left my soup untouched and cold. Because I was so wrapped up in my own little brain I didn't realize I still had my hospital family badge on and Octavia noticed it.

Chris is someone who makes immediate friends with anyone he comes into contact with. He can have a meaningful conversation with someone he just met at the drop of a dime and I love this about him. It drastically compensates for my inability to think of a single thing to say in such situations. They got to talking and Octavia learned that we had just walked there from the hospital to bide time while our son was in surgery. She knelt down next to our table and told us she was a boy mom too. She had three sons and a strong faith and after learning that Vinny had cancer and was incredibly ill, proceeded, in the middle of the brunch rush on a Saturday on King Street, to pray fervently for Vinny and for us. It was so touching it brought all three of us to tears. The kindness that can come just by opening up to a total stranger is overwhelming. When she was finished praying for us the manager came over and said that our bill had been taken care of. Our lovely neighborhood family had called ahead. When the manager asked how she would recognize us, my friend said, "She has probably ordered a bowl of soup," and she found us right away. Octavia asked if she could continue to pray for Vinny and stay up to date on his well-being. Social media made all of that possible.

Chris's Facebook post:

> April 10
>
> Matthew 22:36. A man asks Jesus this question: "Teacher, which is the greatest commandment in the Law?"
>
> Jesus replied: "Love the Lord your God with all your heart and with all your soul and with all your mind." This is the first and greatest commandment. And the second is: "Love your neighbor as yourself."
>
> I'm so thankful for Community and our promise of commUNITY through Christ's promise of Grace.

> Just for today continue to look past differences with each other and Love each other with the same support and Love you have provided Vinny. This is our 2nd most important duty.

We were certainly being loved by not only our neighbors, but complete strangers as well.

We got a call from the nurse during our meal that Vinny was out of his surgeries and doing fine. Upon our return to the hospital, we found that the procedure had gone well and we were able to go back in with him. My parents decided it was a good time, if any, to head back to Florida to pack up the house and stopped in on their way out of town. Again, seeing them was like a breath of fresh air amidst the tentative air I was barely breathing. They had a few minutes with Vinny and prayed over him before they started their seven-hour drive home. Since my parents had to go, Chris left to be at home with Chase and his parents. I sat in my rocker chair the rest of the day, listening to the beeping machines, helping with the checks, asking the questions, and listening to the updates every hour or so. Thankfully the rest of the day was uneventful and we continued to wait for his body to heal enough to take him off of life support. Around 11 p.m. I fell asleep as I had for the previous eighteen days.

WHERE WAS GOD?

Where it all started

Our move to South Carolina

Vinny's first birthday

Disney family photo

WHERE WAS GOD?

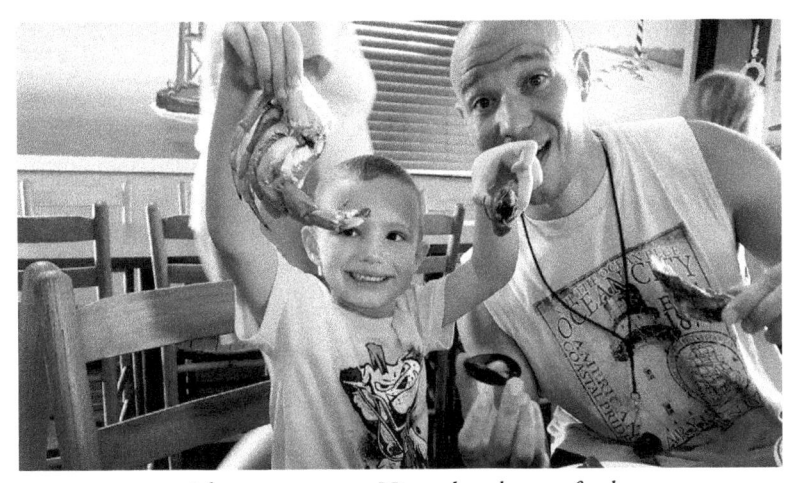

Adventurous eater Vinny loved crazy foods

Vinny in sprinkler in Florida. Pure joy

Me and my boys on the first day of school

The boys playing in the mud after a big storm

WHERE WAS GOD?

Vinny winning at swim meets. He loved swim team but loved the ribbons more

Family photo

> God had a plan long before we did, Grams taught Vinny how to seed marigolds when he was 2!

The Marigolds Vinny planted and cared for with Grams

Family fun photo

WHERE WAS GOD?

Vinny playing basketball

Vinny loved anything fast and exciting

Vinny Sarah Chase and Jake. Best of friends and always four

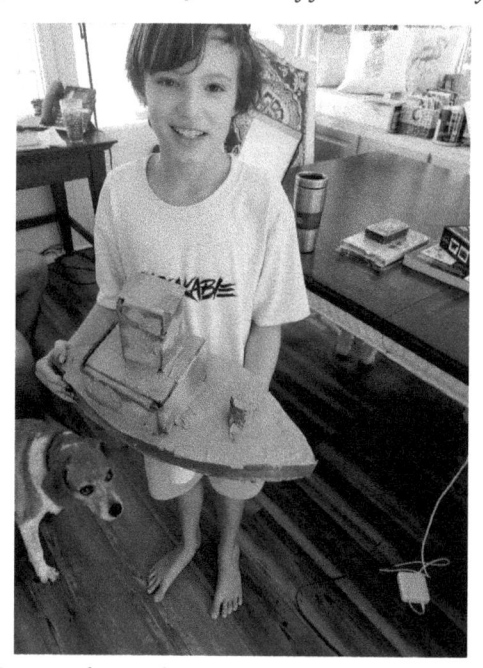

Vinny making a ship. His mind was always working

WHERE WAS GOD?

Vinny with the neighbors dogs. I imagine this for him in Heaven

Swinging in his room

The week before in Myrtle Beach. No hint of Illness except for the now obvious bruises on his legs

The seed Vinny planted in class and a class gift basket

WHERE WAS GOD?

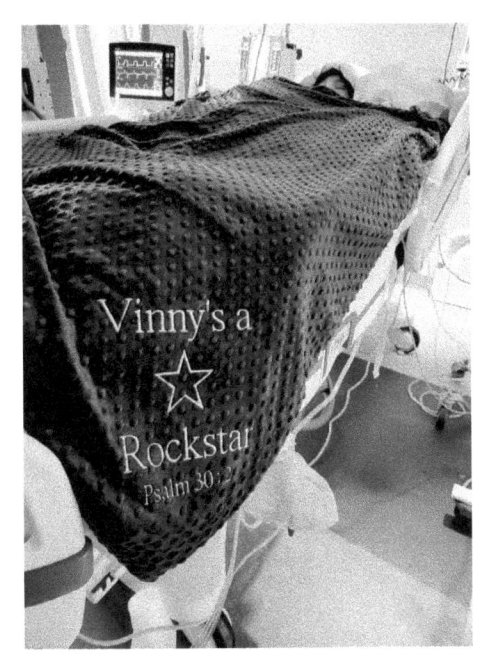

Vinnys a Rockstar blanket

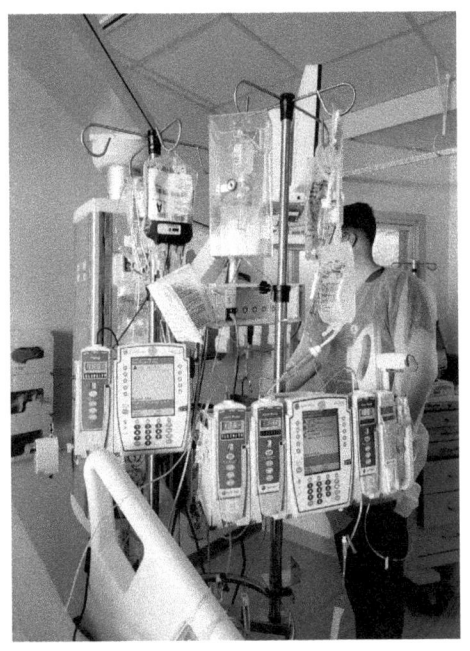

The Christmas Tree

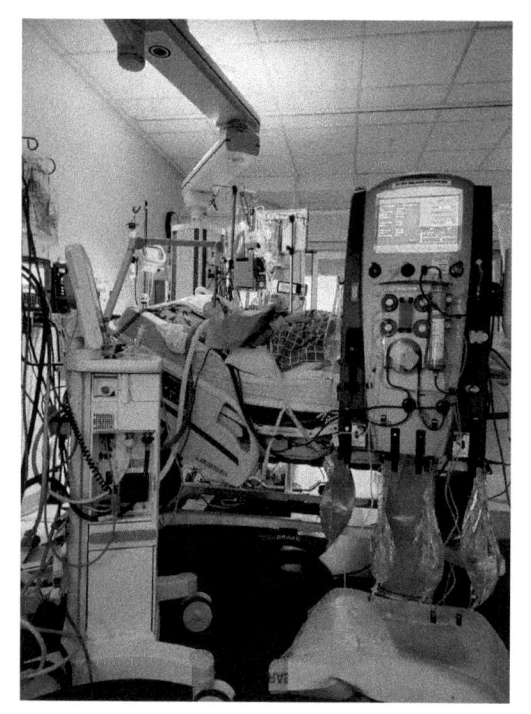

The View from my chair

Vinny Braclets made by Nicole

WHERE WAS GOD?

The Imagine Heaven Book and the Death Certificate on my bed with Vinnys stuffed Dog

All the Soccer Ball Donations

Togo Africa Soccer Team wearing Vinny Jerseys

Jesus Beside Me Image. From all the times I trusted Jesus was right there with us

WHERE WAS GOD?

One of many One Small Seed Box Donations to families in the hospital.

One of the One Small Seed Toy Donations at the Hospital

KIRA TALERICO

My boy

CHAPTER 11

OUT OF MY HANDS

3:15 a.m. The same time I had been waking up on my own, every night we were there, I was gently jostled awake by the head doctor. The nurse that checked his pupils had noticed a deviation. I jumped out of bed. No no no this was not happening. As it was every other time at 3 a.m. in the hospital, the lights were low and the air was cool. It was quiet except for the now reassuring beep of the monitors. The only way to tell if it did in fact indicate a brain bleed was to take him down to CT. Since he was hooked up to every kind of life support, all of the machines and nurses would travel with him. There was no risk of him stopping breathing because at this point the machines were doing it for him. They slowly started making his entire entourage mobile and wheeled him out of the room. No easy feat.

I immediately called Chris. Thankfully Chris's parents were there to stay with Chase and he was able to head downtown immediately. I was worried for his safety knowing he would panic and try to get downtown as fast as possible. From home, my in-laws started to pray. When Chris arrived only a short time later, I was on my knees praying fervently in a completely empty room. He knelt down beside me and joined me in prayer.

April 12

> PRAYERS - They are worried Vinny has a bleed in his brain. Pray that it's nothing and if it is pray that God stops whatever the change is immediately with no lasting effects ASAP

Who would see that post? I had no idea. It was still so early in the morning. I had a frantic feeling that if anyone did, we needed them at that moment. A little while later we could hear the entourage making its way back down the hall. After they wheeled Vinny back in and set the equipment back into place they let us know it would be a bit before the scans were back. Everyone left and closed the door behind them. It was just Chris and me on either side of Vinny's hospital bed holding each of his hands. We said nothing. The glow of the room was warm and soft. At this point it wasn't cold. It was just the three of us and I felt in dire need of God's presence at that very moment. I left Vinny's bedside to turn on some Christian music. Christian music had always been the best way to feel God fill a room and if there was ever a time we needed him, it was now.

By the time I turned on the radio it was 5:15 a.m. and who was on the radio, none other than the pastor who had walked my husband through most of his life, Charles Stanley. A taped sermon of his was playing and so we sat in the quiet with our boy and listened for God to speak to us. And more than I could ever have imagined, He did.

From the voice of Dr Charles Stanley:

> *There are all different kinds of ways to respond to affliction and suffering and hurt and trials and tribulations in our life. Sometimes the simplest thing to do is just rebel against it. Sometimes we choose to very stoically reserve ourselves and just to bear up*

under it. Sometimes we whine and groan and moan and complain about it. Once in a while we may understand what the apostle Paul meant and we may respond the way Paul responded and that is with joyful understanding of God's purpose for allowing that affliction or that pain. I wonder which one of those best describes the way you respond to suffering and heartache in your life.

You know one of the errors that's going around today is that if you pray long enough and hard enough and if you believe enough, then God will change any and every circumstance of life. And that change depends on whether we have enough faith or we pray long enough, hard enough, and intensely enough. Well, if that's true then there's one passage of scripture that we have to look at again. I believe this is the pinnacle passage in all the Bible, the mountain peak passage when it comes to dealing with the grace of God, and how it relates to our pain, our suffering, our heartache, and the hardship that we endure in life. All of us are going to experience those things. It may be physical pain as a result of some disease. It could even be something worse than that and that's emotional pain because of a broken home or the loss of a loved one. Because of loss of finances, because of circumstances and situations that can take a thousand different avenues. There's all kinds of causes of pain.

But what about the goodness of God, poured out without any regards to our worth or anything we deserve? What about this grace of God in our life in the times of pain and suffering and heartache? And what about those things that don't seem to change? Where is the grace of God when you've prayed and prayed and prayed and prayed and nothing happens? When your friends have prayed and you've prayed and you've obeyed God, trusted him, and took your stand and claimed this and claimed that and claimed the other? Where is God?

Well, that's a good question because you see there's a lot of folks in situations and circumstances that don't seem to change and they have prayed. And their friends have prayed. And they've obeyed God and they've done everything they know to do. And nothing's changed. What about the grace of God? Well, that's what I want to talk about and I want everybody to turn to 2nd Corinthians Chapter 12. This is Paul's answer to this very problem. What about my suffering and my heartache and my difficulties and my hardships and my pain when I have prayed and things just don't seem to change. **I'm sure that some of you who are listening are facing that very question.** *"God, I've done everything I know to do and nothing is happening."*

Listen to what the Apostle Paul says. He says in verse 7 of chapter 12, "And because of the surpassing greatness of the revelations, for this reason, to keep me from exalting myself, there was given me a thorn in the flesh. A messenger of Satan to buffet me, to keep me from exalting myself. Concerning this, I entreated the Lord three times that it might depart from me. And he said to me, "My grace is sufficient for you, for power is perfected in weakness. Therefore, I would rather boast more gladly about my weaknesses, that the power of Christ may dwell in me." Then he says, "Therefore I am well content with weaknesses," with insults, with distresses, with persecutions, with difficulties, "for Christ's sake, when I am weak, then I am strong."

Now, either this man is faking us out, or he knows something that most believers do not know! Of course, the unbelieving world could never possibly know. Here's a man who says, I am well content with such things as weaknesses, insults, persecutions, pain, troubles, trials, and heartaches. You name it, he says, I'm just content in all those things.

How in the world can anybody be content in all of that? Grace is God's answer to my pain and affliction and circumstances of life. He may or may not choose to change my circumstances. God does not guarantee to change my circumstances no matter how painful they might be.

Now let's look at the apostle Paul for just a moment. He says, "there was given to me a thorn in the flesh. He says God had allowed this messenger of Satan, brought about this thorn, or this painful experience, that came into his life. We don't know what the nature of it was. It could have been some physical illness. Some people say it was some form of epilepsy that caused him to be depressed at times. Or some say it was an eye disease, or it was some form of temptation that continued to harass him. And so he was forced to deal with or live with what he called this thorn in the flesh.

So the apostle Paul began his ministry and lived with this kind of thorn. ***I want you to listen carefully because I know***

that God has something to say to every single person that hears this message. *Sometimes God will respond to our prayers. Sometimes He will respond to our acts of obedience. In other areas, He will respond and change our circumstances. As a result of our prayer and obedience, sometimes He will. In fact, most of the time He probably does. And so when people say "all you've got to do brother is just name it and claim it, God will do it." Just because He does often and probably most of the time, is no sign that He'll do it all the time.*

And we have a right to say, "well wait a minute now. Does the Bible not say, "ask and it shall be given to you, Seek and you shall find, knock and a door shall be opened to you?" Don't we have a right to expect God to change our circumstances? To take away our pain and suffering and to alter our environment when things get so difficult we just can't stand them anymore? And does He not say in Hebrews chapter four that we have ready access to the throne of grace? That in times of trouble, we can go to the throne of God and receive what we need? Then why shouldn't He change my circumstances when I come to Him and ask Him? Why would God allow me to suffer pain with the hurt of physical and emotional pain? Does He not say in James chapter five that if there's any sick among you let him call for the elders of the church? Let them confess their sins, anoint them with oil, and a prayer of faith will save the sick? I mean all these scriptures imply, and readily, that if I confess and declare that if things aren't the way they ought to be, just talk to God and He'll change them. **Have any of you ever been in a situation where you've prayed and prayed, cried and cried, begged and begged, promised and promised, and Heaven was absolutely dead silent and nothing changed?**

Is this a God of contradictions? Does He make promises over here and fall through over here? What kind of God is this that makes all these promises and then does not come through to change my circumstances. Well let's talk about that. Because brother, that's reality. Anybody who's told you that God will always change your circumstances and always heal you and always make things better and answer your prayer in obedience, didn't tell you the truth. What is it that determines whether God will change my circumstances or not? If it is not my faith, if it is not how obedient I am and how long I've prayed and how intensely I prayed and how sincere I've been, then what ultimately determines whether God is going to change my circumstances or not?

One simple thing. Now listen to this: What makes the determining factor is God's purpose in allowing the pain and suffering and difficult circumstances.

What is his purpose? Look at the life of the apostle Paul. He prayed for God three times to remove this thing and he said God didn't remove it. Now here is a man who had an awesome responsibility. And you would think it would only be right and fair for God to do it. But yet God didn't remove it and to my knowledge there's not a single verse of scripture that said God ever removed this thorn. In the life of Paul the apostle, a great missionary, statesman, and evangelist, there's no sign that He ever removed it. Paul said the reason God didn't remove it was to keep him humble. Now you say "well listen, if God's just telling me to get humble, I will! God doesn't have to send me any of those things to get me humble." Well, that's what we think about ourselves! But you know what? He said, "to keep you from exalting yourself." If you exalt yourself Paul, what you're going to do is ruin my big purpose for your life. Paul, if I don't keep you on your face, if I don't keep you humble, if I don't keep you on your knees, if I don't keep you weak, if I don't keep you absolutely totally dependent you're going to blow the whole thing! **And my purpose is far greater than your individual life.**

Now this is the same man who is saying, "Therefore I am content to boast about my weakness." Four years later he is in prison. He says, "More than all the things that have happened to me that are good, I count all these things to be lost in view of the surpassing value of knowing Christ Jesus my Lord. Who suffered the loss of all things, counted them all as rubbish, in order that I may gain him." He says thorns, stakes, hardships, suffering, beatings, imprisonments, you name it, he says nothing is compared to that. There's something far more valuable to him than God changing his circumstances.

How many times have you and I come to God with some great petition and said, "Lord, now I need an answer." And God answers in three ways, Yes, no, and wait. But then he can say what He told the apostle Paul. My grace is sufficient for you Paul. My love, my presence, my kindness, my gentleness, my provision. Paul, I will be your sufficiency. Paul, My grace, My overflowing, never-ending, inexhaustible, adequate, sufficient, fulfilling, contenting love will be sufficient for your suffering and pain and heartache.

I wonder if that is what God is trying to say to you in the circumstances you find yourself? *That you want so desperately for God to change it. You've made him a thousand promises of what you would do if He would just change your circumstances. Could it be that He has something better than changing your circumstances? And you say, "Now wait a minute! Don't tell me the stuff about being content in my circumstances and my suffering and my pain." Well let me ask you this? Do you think one bad circumstance is all you're going to get in life? You're just going to suffer one time in life, is that all? All of us are smart enough to know that suffering and disappointment are just a part of life. That's the kind of world we live in. There may be some circumstances in which God knows it is better for me to be in that inescapable situation, in order* *for Him to accomplish in my life what He desires. That was true of the Apostle Paul and are we above the Apostle Paul?*

So those people who say "Now listen, if your faith gets right, all you've got to do is name it and claim it! God's going to answer it! God is obligated to answer your prayer! He certainly is. Yes, no, wait, be My guest in the pain. It may not be what we want. If I say to Him, "change my circumstance, It'll strengthen my faith! Won't this strengthen it even more? That while your circumstances don't change and in fact they may even get worse and worse. That the pressure may even become more and more intensified. That the circumstance may be such that not only is it pressure, but it's continual harassment. It may just get worse and worse and somehow there is this awesome sense of indescribable, perfect peace.

Which is the greatest reward? Which is the greatest answer to my prayer? That God has to remove something in order for me to be at peace? Or for God to be within me, while the things that steal my peace, can steal it no longer.

In that moment it was as if God had spoken directly to the depths of our hearts. That at the worst possible moment of our entire lives God was clearly saying, I am here and this is My will. It was like a final sounding trumpet to the race we had been running. And if that didn't make His answer clear enough, the song that came on next confirmed what we believed God to be saying.

Can I believe when I don't see? Can I really let it be out of my hands? When it's out of my hands?

This isn't what I'd choose, but it's where I'm finding You.

When I'm broken and undone, Your mercy's just begun.

You overcome my doubt, Your hands are reaching out.

*You hold me through the storm,
and I will fear no more.*

*I'm not giving up, I'm giving in, to
what You've planned for Your glory.*

At this moment we both knew, beyond a shadow of a doubt, that God was telling us it was time for Vinny to go to his heavenly home. The doctors and nurses had left us alone there at five o'clock in the morning for a full thirty-five minutes. It was the longest we had gone in eighteen days without someone coming in or out of the room. God had created a space, in our most dire moment, to hear straight from Him what His answer to our numerous questions were. "My grace is sufficient for you, for My power is made perfect in weakness." We clearly knew that Vinny was not to be healed the way we had hoped.

As I looked above the bed, out of the closed glass doors and into the dimly lit hall, I saw our team of oncologists filter into the bay around the nurses station. They were standing there, outside of our room, hunched over a monitor. None of them had been at the hospital through the night and in the past they had said that they would be the ones to give us any major news.

As they slowly opened our glass door and came into the room I said, "It's ok. We already know." Doctor Anca gave a small nod that it was in fact the end. Chris and I hadn't said a word since hearing Charles Stanley speak but with only the assurance and inexplicable peace that God can give, we both knew that it was time to say goodbye. The doctors said we could have as much time as we needed with him. Chris laid in the bed with him but I just couldn't. I sat there staring at this face, holding his hands in what I can only describe as a calm state of shock. We prayed and told him how much we loved him, how brave he was, and that it was ok to go home. As we held his hands the nurses slowly shut down each of the machines until there was only a peaceful silence in the room. I didn't understand why as it was happening, but I put my hand on his chest and felt his heart slow to a stop. My poor little man was gone.

We sat there holding him for a few more precious last moments. I lifted my hand up to his hair to stroke it gently off his face and like a painful spike to the heart, it started to fall out just then into my hand. He would never have to go through losing his hair or waking up with his body so physically changed by the effects of the cancer.

Chris got up first but I just couldn't bring myself to leave his side. I knew that this would be the last time I would ever see him and it all felt so surreal. But God had made it clear. And in the midst of devastation, that had given me a small sense of peace. This was God's choice. There was nothing more that could be done. He would never have to climb that insurmountable mountain back to physical health. Slowly, eventually, I could feel that he was gone. He wasn't there with us anymore and it was time for us to leave him. I laid his hand on the bed and moved away.

As I backed away from the bed the doctors were there, all in tears with hugs waiting to embrace me. What happens after a moment like this? After eighteen days of pure physical torture for him, and emotional torture for me? We have to pack up his things and what? Just leave him behind? There is nothing more wrong than leaving a hospital a short time after something so monumental has happened, but our time there had ended. They brought in a cart for us to load up eighteen day's worth of living material, gifts, mail, and who knows what else.

Chris had started gathering the packages, the ones we were waiting for him to wake to open, and started loading them on the cart. There wasn't much room in our tiny living corner so we were using the space under our cot as storage space. As I pulled the last box out, I reached way in the back and grabbed onto the last item under the bed. Vinny's red shoe. The one he had walked in wearing. The one he had worn for months and before that the exact same shoe in a smaller size. They were red Adidas with black stripes and they were his favorite. He wore them down with his wheelies and dragged them on skateboards. He wore them well and he would never wear them again. At that moment it was like a flood of grief hit me in the chest. The reality of the situation bore down on me with unfathomable pain. I clutched his poor little red shoe to my chest as I sobbed. Chris saw what I had pulled out as he turned from loading the boxes onto the cart and crumpled down next to me at the sight of his shoe. We sat there together in a brief moment of torture and cried for our son.

We forced ourselves to gather the rest of our things and as we were loading the last item onto the cart, Benjamin walked in for his morning shift with tears in his eyes. He immediately embraced Chris and I. He had been off the entire weekend but said Friday night he woke up in a panic and felt that something wasn't right. The feeling held all weekend and he worried. He had arrived Monday morning to see that his little patient had passed. When he saw the update of Vinny's passing at the arrival time in his shift, he took a brief moment to himself. In his words, "I may have lost it for a few minutes." He gathered himself together in the midst of his own grief to meet us in ours. He cried with us for a few minutes and I can say nothing about what was said except for the fact that it felt like he genuinely understood the pain we were feeling. He said "I have never seen another parent make the decision you guys had to make with the firm assurance that it was the right one. I have never seen such a solid front from parents before this." He assured us as he walked us to our car that he would take great care with Vinny's body. I knew that Vinny would be in good hands with Benjamin.

AFTER

CHAPTER 12

A THORN IN MY SIDE

Faith doesn't always take you out of the problem. Faith takes you through the problem. Faith doesn't always take away the pain, Faith gives you the ability to handle the pain. Faith doesn't always take you out of the storm. Faith calms you in the midst of the storm.

- Pastor Rick Warren

Monday April 12, 2021

It is with great sadness that we tell you
Vinny went to be with Jesus this morning.

> We know this was God's will and at the time, God spoke to us. We may not have gotten the answer to the prayers that we wanted, but we knew it was his time. He is healed by the blood of Jesus.
>
> My grace is sufficient for you, for my power is made perfect in weakness. Therefore I will boast all the more gladly about my weaknesses, so that Christ's power may rest on me.
>
> Like Paul, I will forever have a thorn in my side. We love you sweet boy.

I think God gives us this state of shock when something so devastating happens. It's like a holding area where the true grief is held at bay for just a little while. Even Benjamin mentioned a state of shock as we made our way out of the hospital. You can cry and laugh with loved ones, tell stories and embrace the kindness of those who love you. I think God holds the real pain at bay for the time when to-dos have stopped and life gets back to a well-known grief term I despise: "your new normal."

I floated through this period. I was fully present but the memories drift in and out as if I wasn't really there. While every second, every sound, every detail of just a few hours before was engraved on my heart with such clarity, the time in "the after" is fluid and memory-like.

On the thirty-minute drive from the children's hospital to our home in Mount Pleasant, we sat in silent tears. My husband was brave and caring even in that moment. He called his parents and let them know that Vinny had passed and that we were on our way home. But I couldn't make any calls. I wanted to shout to everyone around me what had just happened but that familiar vice in my throat wouldn't allow me to utter a word. So like a coward I texted my loved ones. I couldn't bear to hear their voices when I told them that Vinny was gone, let alone utter those unconscionable words. After Chris called his parents he called one of his lifelong friends. Someone who had basically been another uncle to Vinny. When Chris told him that Vinny was gone, I heard his outcry through the phone and the pain he felt at receiving the news. It's a sound I will never forget. My own grief was one of shock and silence. To be able to let out such raw emotion was something I envied and admired. I could feel that same outcry screaming in my consciousness and sitting in the pit of my stomach but for some reason, that's where it stayed for some time.

When we got home, we told Chris's parents and cried together. In the car I kept thinking, how am I going to tell Chase? How do you explain to a seven year old that his big brother went to the hospital and is never coming home? Will he understand? How will he take it? What will this do to him? Chris and I headed up to his room together and sat on the bed. He was just laying down and watching his cartoons. When he looked at us it was with glee. This is the first time both of us had been home in over three weeks. His first question after curiously looking around the room was, "Where's Vinny?" In his little mind, it was all over and we were all back home again safe and sound. I said, "Chase, Vinny went to Heaven." He laughed a little bit and looked between us expectantly, thinking we were joking. We tenderly told him that it was true, that Vinny had passed and wouldn't be coming home. With a bit of a confused look he slowly said, "okay." After a few seconds' pause he quietly said, "Can I watch my show now?" We both responded, "Of course you can buddy," and we left him to go back to his show. I will never forget the look on his face. Bewilderment maybe? Even though he was only seven, he was old enough to understand, but not really old enough to completely comprehend. We were told later that he was in that sweet spot, age-wise. Most of the time kids his age accepted what happened without the mature knowledge that older siblings have. He would either continue that way, with quiet acceptance or at some point in his older adolescence he may start to ask questions. Only time would tell.

It wasn't long before we were surrounded by our neighborhood family. Faye and Justin came first and Faye and I shared a few moments of sorrow and shock. We were sitting in my bedroom and as I handed her some toilet paper to dry her eyes, after years of me telling her my toilet paper was better than hers, she said "this really is better toilet paper," and we both erupted in a teary laugh.

I hadn't seen anyone in the weeks I had been in the hospital and in the next moments I found myself sitting in my favorite chair, in the corner of the living room, surrounded by my wonderful friends. There was a comfort there, in my chair, surrounded by loving women. I remember telling them brief details about what had happened that morning. I remember Jessica sitting at my feet and I tried on her always fabulously sparkly sandals. I remember Faye handing me food throughout the day and constantly telling me to take a bite. But to be honest, even though my stomach growled, the thought of eating was painful and, well, just not important.

The next moment we were all sitting at the table, myself at the head. Justin had provided this wonderfully generous spread from one of our favorite sandwich shops for everyone. Another plate of food in front of me. More conversations, myself mostly quiet. As I looked around the table, Faye at one side, Sarah next to her, and Jake and Chase on my other side, it was another painful silent realization and I uttered, "There should be four. There should always be four," as tears streamed down my face. Faye grabbed my hand and said, "I know honey. I know there should be four," and then promptly sent the three out to play as we sat there and silently cried. There had always been four kids with us. Two and Two. Two older, two younger. Two with her, two with me. Two to switch. But there were always four kids.

There are words that we receive that are forever etched on our hearts. My Bible study mentor Kathy (my 4 a.m. friend as I had mentioned before) and her husband Ray, Chris's Bible study mentor, had asked to meet with us the day after Vinny passed. They had such kind words for us and wanted to make sure we knew they were there for us if we needed additional support as a couple. Kathy had a specific word from God for me. It was, "Job well done, Mama. Job well done." As a mother, your one job is to keep the kids alive. That's the bar. And I had failed. How could I not have seen the signs? How did I not know my son was dying? Why didn't I push that first doctor to run some tests,

ANY TESTS? Why didn't I see the bruises for more than they were? I had FAILED at protecting my child. The words she spoke went directly into that condemnation. I realized those were questions my heart was asking and God had given me an answer that I didn't even know I needed to hear. I had done everything I was capable of doing and beyond that, God was in control.

As much as I knew those questions were not true, I still felt them deeply and daily. I knew that God had shown me, beyond a shadow of a doubt, that it was Vinny's time and he made it clear that there was NOTHING I could have done to change it. After all, his brain was the safe part. The part unaffected by cancer. The last system in his body that was unharmed after every other organ failed. Ultimately it was a brain bleed, the destruction of who he was as a person, that took him like a snap of the fingers. It was a clear "NO." We watched the best doctors in Charleston literally throw the kitchen sink at him and they couldn't prevent his death either.

Still, those words of condemnation crept in. How could you, mom? Even with all that, you still should have caught it before it was too late. For Kathy to say those words, saying that God wanted to tell me "Job well done, mama, job well done," spoke deep into my soul. I had done the best

I could and even though he still passed, I had stood by his side through all of it. There are parts that I regret for sure, but it felt as if God had seen me in those moments, and He knew that I did the best I could and acknowledged it. For someone who is prone to guilt and constantly afraid of being responsible for hurting another, these were the exact words that would stop that in its tracks. They came from someone who I trusted. I trusted her word from God, and it meant everything. To this day those words still bring peace to my heart and tears to my eyes especially when the doubt and condemnation creeps in. Because it still does.

On the southern side of the country, my parents were dealing with the news of the loss with a house full of Small Group friends. As already planned, they were all supposed to help finish packing the entire house for their move to Charleston. Because of the unfathomable turn of events, it was completed in a frenzy. My mom found herself in a similar daze, as somehow her things made it into boxes. My Auntie Debbie and Uncle Russ came over with a box of Kleenex as soon as they heard the news. They all spent the morning in tears and hugs saying, "I can't believe he's gone." Their Small Group friends put a team in every room and did an amazing job helping them pack and label all of the boxes. Auntie Debbie brought food for the entire group and continued bringing things the rest of the week. When the house closed they left in two cars and headed back to Charleston. For an entire year after, they weren't sure where anything was as it was all stacked in boxes in our back room.

As I mentioned, I think God gives us a grace period between shock and grief. A time to get all the things done. A time to be with friends and family. A zombie-like numbness as far as true emotions go. I am grateful for that time that is ignorant of the true depths of grief. Because of it, I was able to be present with our people.

They came from all over. We had planned to have the memorial on Friday and many of our friends and family came in to support us. I could tell you all about how we had to plan for the final arrangements for his body, and the awful events that everyone who has lost someone has to travel through. But honestly it's just too sad. Especially when it's a child. Undeniably when it's YOUR child. So I am going to spare you that part. Maybe my ability to stuff down or block out is overly successful but the small details of that week seem hard for me to pinpoint anyways.

We had a private service for friends and family at our church and we were waiting in the family room before the service. While sitting with one of our pastors, I wanted to get his take on the vision I had of Jesus. He said that while he had no doubt that Jesus had given me a vision, he didn't think that the reason was because Jesus was reaching down to bring Vinny home. There was nothing in the Bible to support that ever happening. With the question still unanswered we went into a beautiful service that we ended with the Pittsburgh Blessing song. Our friends and family had sent up so many prayers for us while he was sick and we wanted to give one back as a thank you.

We also decided that we wanted to do something for the community and the children at Vinny's school. So many people were following and praying for him, and dropping off meals and gift cards and toys and things for Chase, so we wanted to have a Celebration of Life for them. Faye and Nicole, my childhood best friend, ran with my wishes and made everything happen in such a beautiful way. I didn't have to lift a finger. We had the event at the neighborhood soccer fields, where Vinny had played so many times, and over 350 people came from our community.

A few years before, when we were living in Pittsburgh, a wonderful couple we knew had lost their son tragically. In fact, I was pregnant with Chase at the time and so having boys of my own, I felt tremendous grief for this family. Their son had loved trucks and at the funeral they requested guests to bring toy trucks in lieu of flowers. They would be donated to children in need.

When we arrived at the funeral home for their service, the receiving line was twenty feet out the door. We slowly followed the line, through each of the sitting rooms, and every hallway, because so many people were there to pay their respects. They took up the entire funeral home. The most amazing sight was that every single tabletop surface, and along every wall, were piles and piles of toy trucks. There were thousands of them. Such kindness and support was overwhelming to see. The magnitude of emotion at seeing all of those trucks filling every free surface left a lasting impression on my heart. It brought a small good out of a massive loss. I was inspired to do the same.

With the help of social media and the friends at our church, we requested soccer balls to be donated in Vinny's honor at the celebration. Vinny loved soccer. He had played on many teams over the years and was just at an age where he was starting to take notice of the professional players. He even played soccer every day at school and dressed up as the professional soccer player Cristiano Renaldo for his final school presentation. This would be a tribute that he would have loved and a way for the community to get involved. We had planned to disperse the soccer balls into the local Charleston Community, wherever they were needed.

The ladies did such an amazing job at the celebration. I really had no part in the planning besides telling them what we wanted. They had drinks and snacks set up, along with one of the local soccer coaches donating his time to teach drills to the kids on the field. Vinny's teachers stood up and said wonderful things about him and our Pastor brought it all back to God. Over seven hundred soccer balls were donated in the course of one week! We emptied all of the local sports stores and it was enough to fill an entire box truck. The ladies from our church made sure there was a "V" in blue on each ball and then did the amazing task of distributing them to local schools, centers, and programs that might need some new soccer balls. A bunch even went to a program in Togo, Africa where our church does missions. The African team dedicated their entire season to Vinny and had his name printed on their jerseys and I could see God's hand in all of it.

CHAPTER 13

UNANSWERABLE QUESTIONS

Suffering doesn't mean you're cursed, suffering means you're human. The question never is if you understand the why of your suffering. The answer always is how you are going to stand up and walk through your suffering."

—*Pastor Furtick of Elevation Church*

Meanwhile, at home, our lives were unrecognizable. When all of the "events" of someone's passing are over, and everyone goes home, I think that's when God allows for the true mourning to start.

I was talking with Nicole one afternoon, telling her about my vision of Jesus and how I couldn't figure out its meaning and she had the best interpretation of it. She said "I think God was preparing you for what was to come. You were sitting in the position of Mary, under the cross, looking up at her dying son. I think God was preparing you for Vinny's death." Her words hit a chord of truth deep in my heart. That would explain why, in the days after that event, my ever-flowing energy was gone, why I had a sense of foreboding, why the vision was ominous but peaceful. I think she was right. I think God was preparing for me as a mother to lose my precious son. God let me know that He was there and would help me through it. There was a connection to Jesus and the suffering of a son to my loss. The entire time in the hospital, the thought of Vinny's death was unfathomable, but deep down my soul knew that things had changed. This was why I suddenly had the feeling that the mountain he had to climb felt insurmountable, just to get back to a point of health. I wasn't sure if he could do it. It was because he wasn't supposed to.

For weeks after, I couldn't get my head out of the hospital. It was like I was experiencing his death over and over again, night and day, every moment, as if my brain was trying to make sense of what I had seen. As much as I wanted it to stop, and to be able to think of Vinny before he got sick, I was stuck in an endless loop of the eighteen days we had just experienced. I felt DRAWN to the hospital. Here I was, this artist, who had just completed a crash course in every lifesaving medical treatment, medication, and all of the care that goes along with it. The experience of it all filled my brain. There was no existing space for me to mentally file it, so it just went round and round. My grief counselor had said that when someone feels "stuck" in a trauma that they have experienced, that the brain is still processing the information. I will never forget one of the plaques she had on her wall. It said "Grief is our minds spinning from the **constant, relentless assault of unanswerable questions**." Never was a truer statement said. It was constant. It was relentless, and there were no answers to the questions I had.

I felt different too. Darker. My parents were fully moved into our house and it was a blessing. When I couldn't even consider making meals, my mom took over completely. She did all the laundry. All the shopping, cleaning, and cooking. It was a true blessing because I honestly don't think I would have even remembered to do any of those things. She would tell me later that this was her way of helping me when I didn't know how to help myself. Taking control of the house helped her feel some sort of control when it felt like our world was falling apart.

I'm very much a "why" person. Not as in, "why did this happen?" I truly never needed an answer to that question. I knew that I would never get one this side of Heaven and any answer I did get would never help me to understand. More on that topic later.

I am a "why" person as in, if you tell me a fact I will only hear it. But if you tell me why or how it is important I will understand it. Reading and researching became my only outlet for understanding. As if I ever could. (That and eleven seasons of *Grey's Anatomy*. As I said, I had a strong pull towards all things medical.) Every other TV show or everyday event made me ANGRY. It felt so useless and trivial. Things that I'd loved before to pass the time became completely obsolete and superficial. I couldn't even stand to be in the same room when the TV was on without wanting to scream.

I dove into medical research about AML leukemia, at least what I could get my hands on via the internet. Statistics and comparisons about how he could have died so swiftly. Was that normal? Was he just an unlucky anomaly that 60-some percent of kids with AML live? In fact, no. AML leukemia is deadly and often it is quick. I researched ECMO and statistics of survival. The statistics of a brain bleed in particular. This is what claims the lives of most of the patients on ECMO. I even found a study that said fixing a brain bleed via surgery meant that they had to be removed from ECMO to operate on the brain. The statistics of patients taken off ECMO, to endure brain surgery to fix the bleed, were 100 percent fatal. As in, no one survives. The purpose of ECMO is to give the depleted heart time to heal while it pumps the blood in place of the heart. When you take a patient off ECMO prematurely, to fix its complication, the heart is not yet ready to resume its normal function and the patient dies.

A friend of mine named Jenna, one of the Women's Ministry leaders from our church, had dropped off the book *Imagine Heaven* by John Burke. This fit perfectly into my need for research and information because the entire book is a collection of near-death experiences and what the people had seen when their bodies gave out, here on Earth. I read it voraciously. In fact, at the time, it was literally the only time I felt I could breathe. Unlike my usual speed-reading style, I tried my best to read it slowly, so that I could consume every detail and give it a chance to take root and fill this void in my chest.

About a week after Vinny died, while consumed with my confusion of how it could have happened, God sent me the final seal, Vinny's death certificate. I couldn't open the envelope for hours but finally, while alone in my room, with the *Imagine Heaven* book on my lap, I had the courage to open the dreaded manila envelope. There's nothing so real as seeing an official government Death Certificate with your child's name stamped below. I needed to know everything. Reading it was pure torture but I still needed to know. As I slowly read the lines one by one I came to the cause of death section.

> MANNER OF DEATH: Natural
> CAUSE OF DEATH - PART 1
> Septic Shock, Acute Respiratory Distress Syndrome, Acute Myeloid Leukemia
> OTHER SIGNIFICANT CONDITIONS - PART 2
> Acute Renal Failure, ECMO Cannulation, Systemic Heparinization, Nontraumatic Intracranial Hemorrhage

Seven. He had SEVEN Causes of Death and leukemia wasn't even #1. As I sat there reading this list of shockingly serious conditions it was like God was clicking the puzzle pieces into place in my heart. His entire body was compromised. Every single one of those seven things caused his death and the doctors had tried to address each one of them. Even if we would have chanced taking him off ECMO to do brain surgery, his lungs were still severely ill. If all of the antibiotics known to man had cured the septic shock, he was still in renal failure. And if ALL of those things had been addressed and solved, he still had CANCER and could have gone through twelve months of chemo to still succumb to the disease. God placed the words on my heart that were final. Heartbreaking. But the idea that I could have changed any of it was naive. Seeing those seven factors listed on the page were almost comforting. Not in a "feel good" sort of way. But in a way of understanding. God was confirming the choice we made and it was typed out right there in black and white. Even the government said it was so.

That same day I had called his doctors, our first contact since the twelfth. The loop in my head left me with so many questions. I felt I needed some answers, and our doctors were the only ones that could explain them. I had copied Benjamin on the request for a meeting and he asked me if he could join. He wanted to be a "fly on the wall," and having him there was a comfort. After receiving the death certificate, some of those questions were answered. But I still needed to know what happened straight from the ones who had knowledge of each issue.

As the six of us (three of our doctors, Benjamin, Chris and I) sat around the table, I could tell the death of our son had affected them as well. They offered their condolences and we began to discuss some of the specifics of Vinny's condition. In the end, the general consensus was that the leukemia had grown so fast and taken over so quickly that it had compromised his entire system in a very short time. The chemotherapy, the only way to kill the cancer cells, was too strong for his already weakened body and his heart couldn't survive it. Either way, he would have died. After the conversation was over, Chris, Benjamin, and I were talking off to the side and I brought up the death certificate. Benjamin mentioned that he was the one who filled out the paperwork. He knew that I would be reading it and I would see the septic shock diagnosis. We shared a small moment of understanding because of the conversation we had weeks before. There was irony in the fact that it had played a part. But the reality is that sepsis is a common complication.

After the death certificate and meeting with the doctors, I understood medically what had happened but my questions didn't cease. They just turned in a different direction.

Instead of asking "why?" I was asking, "Where is he now? Is he in Heaven?" He was only nine and he wasn't baptized. Sure, we taught him about Jesus and said bedtime prayers. He could recite the Lord's prayer because he had memorized it from preschool at four years old! But he hadn't gotten the chance to choose for himself. He was just coming into the age of learning the possibility of there NOT being a God! When they are so young they just accept it. They know because it's what we raised him to believe. He was just being introduced to the fact that people had different beliefs and at some point he would have to make that choice for himself, but I didn't think he was ready yet.

What is the age of understanding? Is it an actual number or is it just babies who are exempt of judgment? Because every book, reference, and discussion talks about losing babies, but very few have written about losing a school-aged child. What about the fifteen year old who died after a two-year battle with sickness? I don't think she knew God. Is she in Heaven? Would God really send them to an eternity in Hell because they hadn't had the opportunity to accept Him into their hearts at their young ages? Again, my need to research was insatiable. I scoured the internet for direction and ultimately the Bible for the information I was looking for.

How old was the age of understanding? And ultimately, did Vinny make it to Heaven? Everyone I talked to when I broached the subject said "Of course, he's in Heaven! How can you even question that? He's a child!" But Vinny knew right from wrong. He was almost ten. This may seem silly because clearly at ten he had not even begun to live his life on his own terms, but I needed actual confirmation that it was so. God was gratuitous to me for my immaturity in NEEDING an answer to that question. I read all kinds of books and essays and religious writings, but honestly it never says for sure what the age of understanding in God's eyes really is. What I did find in multiple passages in the Bible was that men were not requested of action until the age of twenty. This shows up in a few different books of the Bible under different situations.

> *"Take a census of all the congregation of the people of Israel, by clans, by fathers' houses, according to the number of names, every male, head by head. From twenty years old and upward, all in Israel who are able to go to war, you and Aaron shall list them, company by company." Numbers 1: 2-3*

> *"All who have reached their twentieth birthday must give this sacred offering to the LORD." Exodus 30:14*

> *"This is what pertains to the Levites: From twenty-five years old and above one may*

enter to perform service in the work of the tabernacle of meeting…" Numbers 8:24

"They appointed Levites twenty years old and older to supervise the building of the house of the LORD." Ezra 3:8

"In this wilderness your bodies will fall— every one of you twenty years old or more who was counted in the census and who has grumbled against me." Numbers 14:29

"Surely none of the men that came up out of Egypt, from twenty years old and upward, shall see the land which I swore unto Abraham, unto Isaac, and unto Jacob; because they have not wholly followed me." Numbers 32:11

These were some of the verses I found. NOW, please understand, these are the findings of a mother who has lost her son and is looking for specific answers. Can any of us know the mind of God? No. I don't claim to. There is no age specified in the Bible as a cutoff date for when you will be held accountable for your actions, or a time limit to accepting Jesus, until the end of your time. But finding these verses helped the grieving part of me have something to hold onto. If over and over God did not send men into war, allow them to work in the tabernacle, be counted as those who grumbled against God, or let see the land of Abraham until the age of twenty, then my inference is that those under twenty are still in a "not old enough to be held accountable" zone. Doesn't this make sense? Who of us can think of a teenager who, essentially knows right from wrong, is old enough and worldly enough to have their eternity accounted for! How many of them make terrible, dumb, life-altering mistakes? In fact, it's pretty well known that teenagers make BAD uninformed choices often because of their immaturity. Heck the government's National Institute of Health says that the brain is not even fully developed until twenty-five!

It is well established that the brain undergoes a "rewiring" process that is not complete until approximately twenty-five years of age. This discovery has enhanced our basic understanding regarding adolescent brain maturation and it has provided support for behaviors experienced in late adolescence and early adulthood.

So why would God choose something to the contrary? A God who created us and knows the ins and outs of our minds and hearts. He knows the intricacies of an adolescent mind more than we do because He is the one who created it!

This is my conclusion based on what I have read in scripture. I am not saying that a twenty-one-plus-year-old is doomed. If anything, it made me realize that God wants ALL of His children to make it to Heaven to spend an eternity with Him. Why would he let one of His kids, one who hadn't even had the opportunity to really live, who had their life taken from them before even their parents thought they were able to make the decision to follow Christ, be damned? I think God has the grace to give all of His children the chance to spend their eternity with him. While I may not have a black and white answer to my question, I have been given enough clarity to feel confident that all of our kids, HIS KIDS, are with Him in Heaven.

I know that some will criticize this theory because that's exactly what it is. My theory. What harm does it do but to bring hope to those who have asked the same question about losing their child. But, if you find yourself arguing the opposite, feel free to chime in when you have walked in my shoes.

As one of our current generations' "hovering" mamas, always needing to know exactly where my children were at, I never once had the mistaken feeling that he was missing after he passed. You know that feeling you have when you double check the back seat of your car before you leave it or check their beds at night JUST in case they weren't where they were supposed to be? I never woke up feeling that anxiety of not knowing where Vinny was. I had the sure, bone-deep knowledge, that he was gone from this planet. It was an absolute feeling. As much as I didn't realize it at the time, I think that's why God prompted me to put my hand on his chest. So that my somewhat obsessive control-needing mind would have no question that he was gone. I felt his heart stop with my very fingertips. Even so, that didn't stop my heart from refusing to accept it.

The most physical feeling of loss I had was in my chest. You know that spot when you hold your child and their head rests on your chest? When they are babies, it's where they sleep the deepest. When they are almost your height, it's where their ear rests when they kind of crunch down to give you a hug. It was as if that spot on my chest was abandoned. The longing I felt to hug my child and have his head rest on my chest for just a moment, a shorter and shorter moment the older he got, that spot was empty. Hollow. Void. I never got to hug my baby goodbye. I was missing him deeply and I felt it strongest there on my chest.

Most of my revelations happened while I was sitting on my bed. Always quiet and warmly lit. Painful. Devastating, but safe. This is where I spent my time reading *Imagine Heaven*. In truth, I wish that I had read this book *before* he got sick. I had no idea these experiences even existed to this extent! Story after story of people witnessing life after death, and their stories were eerily similar. Too similar to brush off as coincidence.

You know the Bible tells us to have a Heaven-focused heart, not one focused on the things of Earth in Colossians Chapter three. I could never grasp that concept. I'm not even sure I stopped to think what Heaven would be like. It's a little too sad to think about dying not to mention the fear that sneaks in. It's a little too esoteric to spend any actual time on. I just had the knowledge that one day, far far in the future, I would find out and that was enough for me.

"Heaven is a real place—in fact more real, tangible, and exhilarating than Earth! That's what the Bible has said all along, but I find most people don't have a good image of it," said John Burke in an interview from the Bible Gateway Blog. And now, a piece of my heart was there. It felt like I had one foot in Heaven and the other here on Earth. Part of my soul had left me to waste away here on Earth without it. At least that's what it felt like. Reading this book gave me hope. It gave me visuals and thoughts about what Heaven would be like. Maybe even what Vinny had experienced.

If you haven't read the book, John Burke dives head first into research about Near Death Experiences (NDEs) after the passing of his father. In the book he talks to people from different paths of life, religions, countries, ages, and ethnicities, and tries to witness commonalities about what people experienced. Many of the people saw their bodies below as they hovered above themselves. "Was Vinny there in the PICU the morning we said goodbye? Did he see us say goodbye?" I wondered. Most of them said that there was no feeling of fear or doom, that they realized it was them below but it was inconsequential to the feeling of warmth and pure peace and light that followed. Was Vinny scared? He's all alone up there. I sincerely hope that he had that feeling of warmth and peace and light. Many talked of long tunnels that they traveled in with beings of light leading the way before reaching their destination. They were mostly similar experiences with different descriptions and interpretations. Did Vinny have an angel with him leading the way? Showing him that it would be ok and that he wasn't alone?

What stood out to me most was about WHO they met when they died: angels, loved ones, and ultimately a being of effervescent light and love. This being of light, a man with eyes of fire and a robe and sash (described repeatedly that way) radiates love and a feeling of home. This is exactly how Jesus is described in the Bible. Is Vinny in His presence? Is he safe and thriving next to God?

The only two people I have lost to Heaven are my aunt and my grandmother. Would he know them? He was very little when we lost my Aunt Pam and we only saw Nana every year or two since she lived in Florida. I know both she and Nana would be waiting for him but would he recognize them? Would he feel comfort? Some of these stories talk about people who recognized family members that they hadn't even met!

This book helped give me a visual representation of Heaven. It had always been in black and white in the Bible, but now it was in color in my mind. I tried to take it slowly. One chapter at a time, not race ahead and to let things sink it. All I wanted to do was read that book. When I read it I felt this much-needed peace and calm, as if God was with me.

here is a whole section in the *Imagine Heaven* book that shares visions of what Heaven actually looks like. Multiple NDEs describe seeing a perfect turf like grass with no blade out of place, and pastures of two-foot wildflowers with colors, indescribable in earthly words, that never die, they just bloom right back in place after being picked. Many of them describe the same shimmering light that surrounds everything and majestic mountains that frame a beautiful city. They talk about a crystal-clear stream flowing from a city.

They describe a gleaming city of glass and gold and with streets and streets of large houses! All of this is described in the Bible, but some of them had never even seen a Bible, being from different walks of life, religions, and backgrounds.

One of the closest-hitting chapters for me describes what the walls of Heaven will be made of. The verses are found in the book of Revelation.

> *"The wall was made of jasper, and the city of pure gold, as pure as glass.*
>
> *The foundations of the city walls were decorated with every kind of precious stone. The first foundation was jasper, the second sapphire, the third chalcedony, the fourth emerald, the fifth sardonyx, the sixth carnelian, the seventh chrysolite, the eighth beryl, the ninth topaz, the tenth chrysoprase, the eleventh jacinth, and the twelfth amethyst.*
>
> *The twelve gates were twelve pearls, each gate made of a single pearl. The great street of the city was of pure gold, like transparent glass." Revelation 19-21*

When I read this I immediately gasped. This is exactly what the people in the *Imagine Heaven* book saw. For me it was deeply personal. Vinny loved all things gemstones and mining. He had a collection from all our travels on his dresser. Pieces and pieces of gleaming natural stones were his prized possessions. We had mined for them together! I could just imagine him walking up to this gate and seeing all those levels of glistening rock and the bright smile that he would have on his face. I could just imagine him reaching out his hand and touching the single pearl gate with all of its swirling colors. And the gold streets!! Oh my goodness he would literally and figuratively be in Heaven! The thought of it still makes my heart skip a beat. I can't wait until the day he can show it all to me. When I read those words I felt like God had given me a small glimpse into what Vinny was experiencing. But even all that doesn't take away the pain, the absence, the grief, and the reality of missing my child.

CHAPTER 14

BE BOLD

Be merciful to me, Lord, for I am in distress; my eyes grow weak with sorrow, my soul and body with grief.

Psalm 31:9

A few weeks later, while I was still desperate in my search to find out where Vinny was, and how it had all gone so wrong, a past neighbor had messaged me to send her condolences. Kelly had lived on our street for a while, and I had spoken with her quite a few times about her journey. Believe me when I say it was a tough one, but God spoke to her in a dream, in her teen years, when she was at her lowest. She held on to what God promised in that dream and against all odds, and challenging things thrown at her in between, it had come true thirty years later. Because I knew her story, I believed the dream she had received was in fact from God.

I think God talks to people in all kinds of different ways. With Kelly it has come in the form of dreams. Another friend gets clear images. With me, it feels like more of a whisper or sometimes a vision. When Kelly messaged me this time, she said that she had had a dream. She was sure God had sent it to her for me. She was tentative about sharing it with me and even debated not sending it. Everywhere she went she kept hearing "Be Bold," so she trusted His word. This was her dream.

> *Two nights ago I had this dream/vision of you and Vinny in front of this* **brilliantly lit cloud-like tunnel**, *and you were rushing to Vinny. He was a young man, strong and vibrant, and still looked like the ultimate Prince Charming. His bright eyes were shining with so much knowledge and wisdom, but also held great peace and comfort. He scooped you up in a giant hug and twirled you around. You were overcome with emotion.*

*You had so many tears but still pushed him back so you could see his face. You tried to speak, like you had so much to tell him, but no words came out, only a broken sob. Vinny comforted you then said, "Mom, it's ok, I know it all. I've been with you this whole time. I've held your hand a thousand times and you've ruffled my hair hundreds of times. **That feeling you get in your chest when you think of me, that was me hugging you in spirit**. If I wasn't there with you, I was watching over you from right here. You wouldn't believe what the fireworks look like from here! I've seen all of them, every last one. I know you've missed me, but that was just a blink in time. We have everything now, we have eternity. There is no more need to cry." He was so excited telling you this. He wrapped your arm around his and held your hand, and led you into the cloud-like tunnel talking so passionately about so many things he couldn't wait to show you. But I couldn't understand what was said, just mumbled words as if I wasn't supposed to hear it.*

Then I saw Vinny and Chris in the same place. Vinny looked the same as when he was with you and had his arms open wide. He said, "Welcome home Dad!" They embraced in the most incredible man hug. Chris had his hand wrapped so tightly around the back of Vinny's neck, like he never wanted to let go. Vinny comforted him for a long while then said, "It's ok, we have forever now," and he gently pulled back from Chris. He then said, "I have so many cool things to show you that are gonna blow your mind." He tilted his head and said in a teasing way, "I gotta say though, I'm not so sure you can keep up with me now." He held his arms up, kinda posing so Chris could check him out, and started flexing his muscles and laughing. Chris had this shocked look on his face and was like, "Oh, yah?!?!" (like, it's on now buddy) and they walked into the cloud-like tunnel laughing and teasing each other... And just like that, with an overwhelming feeling of peace and joy, you started your eternal life together like only a few days had passed.

It was absolutely incredible Kira! He answered my question and forever changed the way I will look at Heaven and this process, but I truly think this message was meant for y'all. I hope you find meaning in it!

These words brought streaming tears down my face. How could she have known? I hadn't told anyone about that ache or feeling in my chest where I felt the longing the most. After reading this I had so much gratitude. GOD thank you for speaking to me through her dream. It was so specific to our lives and the comfort it brought me was immeasurable. "Now to Him who is able to do Immeasurably more than we can ask or imagine." Ephesians 3:20. This was a verse that was spoken at the end of every church service and here God was, doing the immeasurable. This was one of those moments. This word, however small or unknowing for others, was another deep breath that I could take in a long line of shallow gasps. A true word from God. He had my baby and my baby was ok.

I have told you these things, so that in me you may have peace. In this world you will have trouble. But take heart! I have overcome the world! John 16:33

At this point Chase was still in school and Chris and I would take walks just to get out of the house. People had been occasionally asking if I had any sign from Vinny yet or if I had seen cardinals, etc. On one walk about two weeks after he had passed we walked out of our house to find a bright blue (the same color blue that we did his entire celebration of life in) V on our curb. Apparently the water or electric companies had gone around marking where the lines were and on our entire walk there were bright blue Vs around every corner. This continued for months and now every time I see one I like to think he's on the walk with us. This was my first wink from Heaven.

Faye had always believed that cardinals were a sign from the other side. I was skeptical but she swears that after her father passed, one tried to get into her house for months, constantly tapping on the window. I thought, at best, maybe an angel was using nature to give a comforting sign, knowing our traditions. We were arguing as much out on the back patio when, no joke, a cardinal flew down and sat directly on the chair in front of us. We both sat there in silence staring at it when Faye yelled out, "OH, COME ONNNN!!!" Now, whether that is God's way of comforting us, or an angel, or Vinny himself getting a little smile, I will never know until I'm there myself. Maybe it will bring us a good laugh when we find out the truth! For now, every time I see a cardinal, I get a little smile and think of our conversation. If anything, it gives me a moment's pause to think "What if?" and just in case, I send up a little acknowledgment.

CHAPTER 15

A LONG DEEP BREATH

"You are trying to praise God with a taste in your mouth of disappointment and fear. It is hard to say Hallelujah when your mouth tastes like hurt."

—Pastor Steven Furtick of Elevation Church

"God is close to the brokenhearted." You know, that verse is a true, tangible fact. I felt Him daily. I am a great, put-on-a-smile kind of girl. I didn't show my pain, on purpose, very often, but it was deep to say the least. I once described it as if my heart had been thrown in a blender, and I was just wading through the muck, seeing if there were any pieces that were salvageable. But I rarely let it surface until I was alone. That was the only time I could truly grieve without restraint.

One particular night, the relentless assault was happening yet again; in fact, it loved to plague me particularly at bedtime. At about midnight I snuck out of bed and into Vinny's room. I turned on the light, sat on the floor, and cried. And cried. Ugly, silent, gut-wrenching, soul screaming cries. I couldn't even inhale because the act was so physical and violent it was as if my body was in a spasm of grief. After the wave of grief subsided I sat back against his wall holding one of his beloved stuffed animals. As I looked around the room, I remembered reading that sometimes angels minister to us in times of great grief or pain. At that moment I wondered, are there angels here with me? I could imagine six or seven of them sitting in different spots around the room, heads hung low, somber with me in my grief. I could imagine one sitting on the top corner of Vinny's bunk bed, and another on the dresser. All faced toward me, joining me in my sorrow, and it was a comfort. I can imagine them even today. I like to think that maybe they were really there but only Heaven can tell.

Even though God was showing me moments of hope, I felt physically shattered. At the time I was journaling on occasion, a tip from my counselor. One night, this was all I could write.

Scorched. Black. Like a dry and cracking wasteland. I feel hollow and beaten, broken and bleeding. With every breath, smoke fills my lungs from my scorched interior. And while I may be walking and talking, emotionally I am weak and beaten. Sprawled out on the floor, unable to lift a finger. But you will never know. I will keep my pain buried and private. Alone and dark. Because who could survive being scorched on both the inside and the outside? No one.

Kelly reached out again. She'd had a second dream. In fact, this time, she felt so uncomfortable about it that she didn't message me for a week. In God's humor, it took a red Ford Explorer (my car at the time) following her all around town when she finally said FINE! I'll tell her! This was her dream:

> *I saw you kneeling at God's feet with your head in His lap (much like that Facebook image you shared on Jesus Beside Me) but this time you are sobbing with such great despair in His lap. You were barely able to catch your breath. I swear I could feel your pain and this hollow feeling deep in my soul. God was stroking your hair and consoling you like there was no place else He needed to be; you*

were His only concern. He looked at you as you cried and said, "I know you feel like your backyard is quiet and your home is empty, but I can assure you My "backyard" is anything but." He had this lopsided grin on His face like he was thinking "if you could only see the hell Vinny is raising here in Heaven." Then He looks over His shoulder to His "backyard" and I saw the most **incredible peaceful streams, rolling hills, lush green fields, and majestic mountains, and Vinny was swinging** on vines in this forest (straight up George of the Jungle style). He was screaming at the top of his lungs with such joy. There were so many angels following him, and it seemed like Vinny had reawakened all of them. The whole place was filled with laughter and wild screams of joy, and as you were lost in your pain and struggling to get through it, it was like this is one of God's greatest struggles too. He so badly wanted you to be able to see Vinny, so strong and confident and running with reckless abandonment. He wanted you to see what it is really like on the other side. I *got this feeling that He struggles so much with the pain we feel as humans when He takes a soul home and wants to desperately ease your pain. Then God kind of nudged you and motioned for you to get up. I could see what He wanted you to do in a side picture. He didn't want you to kneel down for Him, but to crawl into His lap and throw your arms around His neck, just like a little girl crawling into her daddy's lap. You were hugging Him and He had held you in His arms. As you cried, every time you exhaled I could see this cloud of grief and pain leave you. He replaced it with a glowing light of His peace, comfort, and strength and it literally just flowed into you. It was like He wanted you to seek solace literally in His arms and let Him fill you with His strength with every breath you took. It was so vivid and beautiful and peaceful. I could literally feel His power in my lungs when I woke up, they were just tingling.*

When I was in a pit of despair God gave me these words. As I read, I found myself taking a long deep breath, imagining that God was filling my lungs with His power, His love, His strength. How great is his compassion for me that he would take the time to show us that scene. There have been so many times since this dream that I have been steadied by a long deep breath, knowing that God was on the other end breathing life into my soul in the midst of despair.

Even though it was clear that God was with me and had shown me all of these wonderfully supportive things, I always needed Him more. After receiving these messages from Kelly, I really wished for my own dream of Vinny. Just to see him one more time. Just to say goodbye since I didn't really get to do that. I pleaded with God to give me a dream. I prayed and prayed for God to show me Vinny. I fell asleep sure that God was going to answer my prayer and when I woke up without any dreams, I felt disappointed and sad. So that next night I prayed again. "GOD PLEASE show me my boy again. I NEED to see him even if it's only in a dream." As I fell asleep this is what I saw…

I am looking down at my bare feet while walking in the sand. So clear, so real. The sand dissipates with every step and I walk out onto a sidewalk in the city. As I am walking, I have this known "task" of picking up my little brother from school. As I walk past a bunch of people bustling about, a man bumps my shoulder and whispers something into my ear as he carries on. I turn to see his face, but I can't hear what he says and he disappears down the street. I continue with purpose as I enter a beige-painted, cinder block computer room, much like you'd see in a school. As I see a boy sitting at a computer with his back to me, I go over and put my hand on his shoulder and say, "Come on, it's time to go." As the boy turned his head, he flicked his hair to the side, just like Vinny did, and looked up at me. As clear as day it was Vinny's face I was looking at. He got up from his chair and went over to the lockers and crouched down to put books in his bag. The realization hit that it wasn't my brother but my child that I was here to pick up. I ran over to him and dropped down to my knees next to him and grabbed his hands. As he stood up in front of me, I noticed he was crying. I asked why he was crying and he said "I didn't even make it past the third grade." I scooped him into my arms and held him so tight with his head on my chest. I hugged him with the understanding that I missed him terribly. As I rocked him in my arms, his head on my chest hugging me back, I started to cry. As I took my last breath I cried, "I have missed you so. I am lost without you, Vinny. Lost without you," and the air left my lungs as those last words whispered away the dream.

That instant I sat up straight in my bed and the grief hit me as if I had lost him all over again. The pain I felt was overwhelming. The clarity of each step, every texture, my surroundings, his face, the way his hair swung to the side of his brow when he turned his head. The way his head felt resting on my chest in one final embrace. It wrecked me. I cried for hours that morning. As grateful as I was that God answered my prayer and gave me one last hug with Vinny, I realized that sometimes God says "no" because it's what's best for us. God didn't give me a dream that first night because He knew it wasn't what was best for me. It would cause me immense pain and heartache and yet I pleaded with Him to give it to me anyways. Sometimes He will give us what we plead for, even when it's not what's best for us, He will answer our prayers and be there with us in the wake. I understand now why God doesn't allow us to see our loved ones after they pass. The pain of it, the loss is more than I could bear. As I laid on my pillow and sobbed, I thanked God for answering my prayer, for giving me one final hug with my son, and asked Him to never show me Vinny again.

CHAPTER 16

WHY? WHERE? WHAT IF?

Aim at Heaven and you will get earth thrown in: aim at earth and you will get neither.

–C.S. Lewis

During the days, as blurry as they were, my social media was constantly flooded with unexpected notes from God. I follow Steven Furtick, the pastor of Elevation Church in Charlotte, NC. I have listened to many of his sermons and each time I felt God addressing some question in my life. His team is great at posting daily and on every social media outlet. I would see posts regularly like:

"God hears your cry because He is near. The righteous cry out, and the Lord hears them: He delivers them from all their troubles. The Lord is close to the brokenhearted and saves those who are crushed in spirit." Psalms 34:17-18

The day I read this post I was struggling, yet again, to hear God's voice. When you feel the closeness of God, you start to crave that feeling, and when I am lost in grief, all I want is for God to show me His face again. I wrote in my journal, "Today is a day when I need Jesus. The last few days, I can't even name what I am feeling. Angry? Lost? Sad? Depressed? Deflated? Exhausted? All or none of the above? It's just a weight, a feeling of unease. Yesterday my body actually hurt and everyone thought maybe I was coming down with something, but truthfully I think it was just grief. I don't let it out and some days it takes over physically. Today my mind is consumed with frustration."

Not knowing where to turn, or how to quench or name these feelings, my Bible called to me. You know how it does when you get this tiny voice that says, "maybe look in your Bible," but something else inside you says, "Nah, that won't help and I don't want to." I decided to try my 365 Day Grief Devotional and sincerely pleaded, "Lord, please speak to me. I need you. I don't know what to do with myself. Show me your face. I need to see it!"

I turned to the entry for that day, the title being "Held by Love," and sure enough, this was the verse: "The Lord is close to the brokenhearted: He rescues those who are crushed in spirit." (Psalms 34:18) The recognition of those words reverberated deep in my bones. That was it. That's what I was feeling. Brokenhearted and CRUSHED in spirit. I had a name to my feelings and God had given me the verse. The text of the day read:

> *Merciful Father, you see me in my brokenness. When I have no strength to even call out to you, you draw near to me in my heartbreak. I have tasted and seen your goodness in my life and I believe I will see it again. But for now, in the depths of pain and grief, you come close and surround me covering me in your love. I trust that you will not let me be crushed by the weight of this anguish.*
>
> *Keep me together Lord, when I feel like I am breaking at the seams. Center me in your kindness. I remember that you don't have any hidden agendas: you love because it is in your very nature to do so.*

I won't hide myself from you or keep you at a distance today. Come in close.

There is usually a question at the bottom of the page and it read, "When you are overwhelmed by sadness, do you believe that God's presence is yours in the midst of it?" God was answering my call and literally saying, "Here I am, and My presence is yours in the midst of your sadness." From there I FINALLY turned to my Bible. There was an unknown, forgotten folded piece of paper holding an unimportant place. When I opened it to see what it was, I realized it was a note one of the nurses had left on my pillow, one night in the hospital. It was a torn piece of scratch paper that said "Don't panic. I'm with you. There's no need to fear. I will give you strength. I will help you. I will hold you steady and keep a firm grip on you." Isaiah 41:10

The amazing goodness of God is that He knew, months before, when this note was written while I was in the hospital during a time of need, that it would also be read in the months after, at this very moment, when I needed him again. He was here, in my room with me, when I was calling His name. In that moment, the weight on my shoulders lifted and I knew I could face yet another day knowing that God was with me. I turned over the scrap of paper and on the back was written "The Lord is with you your mighty warrior." –Judges 6:12. Tears sprang to my eyes and ran down my cheeks as I felt the strength of God fill me up. Something was telling me to read Psalms. I went back to my grief book to reread what had given me strength and realized that the verse that had started it all was Psalms 34:18. "I sought the Lord and He answered me. He delivered me from my fears." It was as if I had started on a path and God led me, at every turn, to show me His Grace. How sufficient He really is in my weakness.

I think a lot of people can get lost in "Why" something terrible has happened. Why did Vinny get Cancer? Why did God do this to me? Why did God allow this to happen? Why didn't God change my circumstance? Why does God heal others but He didn't heal Vinny, not in the way I asked anyway. I swear, if you let that question of "why?" snowball it can consume years of your life. There can be so many whys to so many situations. But do they ever give us answers? Realistically will any answer ever be good enough? No. We didn't get the answer we wanted, and we already know that, so what's the point in asking?

Why did Vinny get cancer? Because we live in a fallen, sick, disease-filled world. Who doesn't have a loved one who has heard that dreaded word, cancer? In fact, there are multiple people in my family alone who have had many different cancer diagnoses. I believe that cancer is our generation's plague. Before they had the black death and smallpox. Now we have a disease that can hit every part of the body and is popping up everywhere regardless of geography, genetics, or economic disposition.

Was this a punishment from God? For my mistakes or the mistakes of generations before me, like it talks about in the Bible? The idea that a punishment is coming, from the mistakes of another generation, is a popular and widely-known belief. Pastor Paul Leboutieller of Calvary Church Ontario has a poignant view on generational curses. 2nd Corinthians 5:17 says, "Therefore, if anyone is in Christ, he is a NEW CREATION. Behold the old has passed away and the new has come." If you believe that Jesus died on the cross for your sins, then you are a new generation and God will show "steadfast love to thousands of those who love me and keep my commandments." (Deuteronomy 5:10) When you come to Christ, He has taken your judgment and condemnation. If you have accepted Him, then past generational curses are wiped clean.

All of these questions that we torture ourselves with are questions that are NOT from God. They are questions from the enemy. They are meant to pull us away from God's light and peace and into a place of anxiety and darkness. I will never know where Vinny's cancer came from just as the doctors didn't. I will never know when it started, but I know for a fact there was nothing I could have done to change the outcome no matter how many times I ask myself that question. God was clear on that. Even if there was something I could have done differently, would it have changed the outcome? No. Because when it's our time it's our time, regardless of what we prayed for or how much we prayed. Only God knows when that time ends.

Some people have the audacity to think that bad things happen because the person's faith isn't strong enough, or they didn't pray hard enough, or they didn't believe deeply enough. In our case, none of those things are true. We did pray hard enough, my faith has always been very strong and I truly believed our miracle would come in the form of physical healing. Assuming that those things can affect the will of God is assuming that we have the power of God to make things happen and we don't. Because sometimes the answer to our prayers is yes, sometimes it's wait and sometimes it's no. God's grace is sufficient, for His power is made perfect in our weakness. I thought, "What better way to show all of those people watching the amazing power of God, through the miraculous healing of Vinny's disease?"

But the answer to our prayers came in the form of healing by way of Heaven. I hope that one day, people will still see the amazing power of God through what we endured. Did God cause Vinny to die? No, cancer did. But can God do good from my pain? I think that's why He showed me His face. So that others could know that God is with them too, in the midst of their trials, even if it's not as obvious as it was for me.

In my voracious need for connection to Heaven, I not only read *Imagine Heaven* but I also read *Proof of Heaven* by Eben Alexander, MD. A story about a neurosurgeon who understands the science behind the brain and consciousness. The book is his story of his near-death experience and how he came to understand that the brain did not come first, consciousness does, and we exist before our physical brains do. It was his experience in meeting God that changed his beliefs from atheism to belief in Jesus Christ. I also read *Waking Up In Heaven* by Crystal McVea, who says, "I was a skeptic and a sinner, and I didn't believe in God or in Heaven. But God is real. Heaven is real. And God's love for us is the realest thing of all."

Additionally, I read *Nine Days in Heaven* by Dennis and Nolene Prince. One of the things that I read repeatedly from different experiences of death was that, not only are you consumed with the feeling of all-encompassing love when you die, but that all the questions you had prepared are already answered. There is no need to get to Heaven and ask God the dreaded "why?" because all will be laid plain. These stories detailed the immediate experience of infinite understanding of all things. An understanding that goes beyond the comprehension we have here on Earth with all of our questions answered. So why spend days, weeks, or even years asking "why" and letting the question poison every aspect of your life, when not only will we never get an acceptable, understandable answer, but the moment we reach the life after this one, all of the questions are answered without even having to ask them.

One of the things that I didn't realize I would grieve for was for Vinny's future. I had prayed for and thought of his future wife, wondered what career path he would take, and what college he would choose. What sports would he be into in high school? How tall would he be? These are all things we think about of our children. I had to grieve what I thought was supposed to be his future. What I didn't understand was that he was never supposed to have one. His life was only supposed to be nine years long. I just didn't know it. There is a movie called *Courageous* that details the story of a father losing his young daughter and at the end he says he had to change his mind from being angry about the future with her he was missing, to grateful about the years he was given with her. I remember seeing that and thinking "Ohhh I don't know. That's a lot to ask of anyone. I don't know if I have that same level of faith." But here I am, dwelling on these same concepts now myself. It is true, once you realize their future, the one you had prepared for was never meant to be, you have to continuously decide to change your mindset to one of gratefulness. This is a day-to-day and even minute-to-minute conscious choice because it goes against all nature, and I don't succeed in many of those moments. But it does help me keep the what-ifs at bay. Why ask "what if" if it was never "meant to be."

I have had many people say, "I don't know how you do it. I could never go through what you are going through, surviving losing a child." And I get it. It is literally every parent's WORST nightmare. It is the one thing we could never understand because it isn't supposed to happen. We are supposed to go before our children in every case. Yet it happens every day in other countries. The reality is, there isn't another choice other than to endure. I know other moms walking the same path and each of us has chosen to keep walking, for our husbands, for our other children, simply because what other choice do we have? You just keep choosing to do it one day at a time. I'm just one more mother trying to navigate grief this side of eternity.

Grieving is for us, not them. I came to a point of understanding that pleading for God to give him back is a selfish plea. I want him back because I am devastated without him. He is a part of me and that part has been cut off. But HE is in a better place, and I don't say that lightly. For him to be there means he will never again feel the sorrow and anguish I feel. He will never be let down or cast aside. He will never have to make the hard choices we all have to make. He will never again feel the physical toll that cancer takes on a human body. For that I have to feel grateful. He is truly in a better place and so when those calls come from my heart I know that they are for me, not for him. Ultimately, he already crossed the finish line to the race the rest of us are still running.

We had so many small notes from Heaven, or God winks, but one in particular stood out. It was Mother's Day no less. My first Mother's Day without my firstborn. This was just a few short weeks after he had passed and I was sitting in my favorite corner chair again, looking out the window, reflecting on the bittersweetness of it all. Bitter being the stronger taste. As I looked out the window on that sunny, southern May morning I saw the little flowerpot with the seedling Vinny had planted in class right before he got sick. The one he was so worried about surviving while he was in the hospital. Right in the middle of his little single green flowerpot was none other than a perfectly formed, newly bloomed, red marigold. It was the most beautiful bloom anyone could ever ask for. Vinny had sent me flowers on Mother's Day. A perfect flower, one that he had planted himself. At that moment the sun was shining, and I could feel warmth like a warm hug from Heaven.

CHAPTER 17

CALL ME MARA

"Stop asking God to take the thorns away that He left there so you would know Him! In my weakness He is strong! If it is not good, then He is not done."

— *Pastor Furtick*

I don't think that I would have the deepness of faith or the hunger for Heaven that I do if I had not walked Vinny's death with him. Will I ever, in a million years, be ok with losing my son? Absolutely not. I would never choose it. I doubt any mother ever could, and I think God commiserates with us and understands the humanness of that reality. We could never choose to give up our children regardless of what it can lead to later on in life. I'm just not capable of that kind of selflessness. But I did go through it, and there's nothing I can do to change it. So what am I to do now?

About eight months into the After, I was tired of talking about grief and wanted to enter a normal bible study with other women in my community. A bible study that would further my knowledge of the word, and not of my dreaded feelings. I went to the online Seacoast Church website and signed up for a study group that was listed to be in the next neighborhood and at the perfect time to fit into my schedule. I wasn't given any other information and waited to be contacted. A short time later I got an email from my now-friend Kim. She invited me to the group at her house and honestly it was a breath of fresh air. What I didn't know was that Kim was the wife of one of the men in a Bible study with Chris years before.

God works in such caring ways. Months before, Kim had seen my picture in the paper for my business called Map Mom. I don't recall that photo, but once she had seen it, she felt this word from God that she needed to know me. She had intended to reach out just before Vinny got sick. Once Vinny got sick she decided to wait until an appropriate time to message me and began to follow along online with Vinny's progress. She told me later that the day Vinny died she cried all day, without even knowing us. She felt deeply connected. They even attended our family service for Vinny's funeral. She wanted to introduce herself to me, but still felt it wasn't the appropriate time. She thought I wouldn't want to hear from her with all I was going through, so she waited. Until such a point that God prompted me to find a random small group online with her leading it. When she opened the email to find out I was the one inquiring, she knew it was God bringing us together.

Shortly after we met, she told me that story. I was so unsure about joining a new group of women at the stage of grief that I was in. A lot of people in our town knew me because of my business and then with what happened to Vinny… well, it was known. Occasionally Chris and I would have people stop us, whether at a local event or the bank even and say, "I know who you are…" and then politely ask to give us a hug or pray with us. So how on earth do I meet new women? Do I come right out and tell them what I am going through, because that's not uncomfortable or TMI at all. Do I keep it to myself and then in a few months when it comes out, they ask why I didn't tell them? When Kim told me the story of how God had worked for months to bring us together, I knew that God had set me up to be with these women at that time. And the fact that Kim had already walked through it with me, even without my knowledge, meant that I didn't need to relive it all for her. She understood my hesitation and helped lead me through it at an appropriate time.

While in our small group, Kim introduced me to a pastor that she and Brad (Kim's husband and Chris's friend) often listened to online. A pastor that would become integral in the growth of my understanding of the big scary Bible, even though he has no idea who I am or that I even exist. Pastor Paul Leboutellier of Calvary Church Ontario in Oregon (not Canada), as quoted before, had been recording his sermons throughout the Bible on YouTube for the past ten years! You can literally pick any book, any chapter, any verse on their website and there is a fifty-minute sermon about the history, the knowledge, the background and the message of said verse, word by word. After referencing him in Bible study a few times and hearing a few of his related messages I began to listen to his podcasts with tenacity. His way of explaining literally every verse in the Bible had me seeing the messages with a clarity I have never seen before. I've listened to Genesis, Exodus, Ruth, Revelation, and now John. It's true that God opens your eyes to understand new ideas in concordance with the growth of your faith. Even when it's the same passage you have heard more than a few times.

It's funny how God uses any and all means to speak to his children. We were coming up on the one-year anniversary of Vinny's death when Pastor Furtick preached a message from the book of Ruth. Late March has become a bleak time for me. It was the start of all of the horror we endured and every March I start to feel a foreboding feeling. As if every day that gets closer to April twelfth, I feel it all over again. The title of the message was "It will come together." At the time, churches were just starting to meet again post-Covid after most of them had been closed and meeting virtually for a long time. A lot of people had been suffering at the same time I was. Their sermon was about the Bible verse:

> *"And we know that all things work together for good to them that love God, to them who are called according to his purpose." Romans 8:28*

His message taught that all things come together for HIS purpose, not MY preference, not MY plan. The book of Ruth tells the story of Ruth and Naomi. Naomi lost her husband and then shortly after, her sons, one of her sons being Ruth's husband. Ruth decided to stay with Naomi when they had to leave because of famine in the area instead of returning to her family. After losing her husband and sons, Naomi said to call her Mara instead because Mara means bitter.

Now as much as I have a strong faith and understanding that this was all according to God's plan, it doesn't mean I understand or like it. I resonated with being called Mara. Pastor Furtick said "this message is for someone who is in a place they didn't plan to go. Naomi didn't plan to go to Moab, to a place she hated." But God said I am with you in your bitterness. He did not hold it against Naomi that she would be bitter from her loss. That was in chapter one of the book of Ruth. Little did Naomi know that a few years later, in chapter four, she would be holding a newborn son, a new family line.

"Stop asking God to take the thorns away that He left there so you would know Him! In my weakness He is strong! If it is not good, then He is not done." said Pastor Furtick.

How is it that a year later, God can still put these same words in my path, through a TV screen, to my ears. Bitter ears that sting with loss and pain. Speaking directly to the thorn I continue to carry in my side. The thorn Charles Stanley said that the apostle Paul also carried. Then he quoted the same Bible verse Charles Stanley had used a year prior. In my weakness, He is strong. But Pastor Furtick added a new concept. "If it's not good, then God's not done."

Naomi's baby ended up being the grandfather of Jesse, who was the father of King David, who ultimately became the line with which Jesus Christ himself came. Naomi's suffering brought out a nation even though she didn't see it in her lifetime. Pastor Steven continued, "How many of you went through something so dark you couldn't even explain how you got through it, but there was grace, wasn't there? If someone would have said you could live through that you would say, 'Just call me bitter. I can't make it. It's over.' But God still knew Naomi's name. He was with her in her bitterness. It will come together, you just gotta trust God in this part, it will come together, if you don't give up."

I was coming up to one year after Vinny's death and I understood those feelings. I felt bitterness. I was angry. I felt all of the things you feel when someone is taken from you. I wasn't specifically mad at God, I was just mad, bitter. And I was fine there in my bitterness. I did not want to leave it behind just yet. Naomi's feelings resonated with me so deeply that I almost bought a necklace with the name Mara on it. Just call me Mara.

I don't know what God has in store for the future, or what our life will look like as the years pass. But I can have faith that, just like Naomi, God will be with me in my bitterness. He will remember my real name and He will work all things together for the good of those who are called according to his purpose, not mine. Even if I never see it in my lifetime. Eventually I will let the bitterness fade.

CHAPTER 18

PATIENT ENDURANCE

"I think a lot of us miss our turn to be used by God because of disappointment in our life and setbacks we've experienced. But, on the other side of disappointment, often we can see that our disappointments led us to our destiny."

—One Minute Message Facebook Post by Pastor Steven Furtick

One of the Bible studies we took on in our small group was the book of Revelation. Being that I was somewhat obsessed with death and the life after, diving into what the end of the world looks like was a near second. The word that stood out the most while reading Revelation was "perseverance." Over and over it tells us to persevere or to patiently endure. Being a Christian doesn't mean that my life will be free of trials and tribulation. But it does call for me to patiently endure those times with the understanding that God is there with us in the pain. To persevere means persistence in doing something despite difficulty or delay in achieving success. Can we patiently endure the heartbreak in our lives *with* the pain?

We all struggle in the wait. Our society tells us that we need answers now. Not in a week, not in a month, and forget waiting decades like they did in the Bible. If we have a need or a want, it needs to be satiated immediately. Otherwise, we should distract ourselves until an answer comes. Still, when we dull our minds with distraction, God gives us grace and finds us in that place. How many times did I open my social media, to escape my current reality? How many endless hours of mind-numbing scrolling did I waste to quiet the torrent of unwanted thoughts? How many times did God meet me in that place?

Many, many times. Verses would present themselves like, "I remain confident of this: I will see the goodness of the Lord in the Land of the Living. Wait for the Lord: be strong and take heart and wait for the Lord." (Psalm 27 13-14) and

"This is how change is: it just shows up at your door and it doesn't ask for an appointment. And we didn't mind the new thing as long as we ordered it off the menu. But God said sometimes you have to make room for the new even if you didn't see it coming. The change in your life might be God making room for a miracle, for breakthrough, for transformation." This was another of Elevation Churches posts. There were so many more. A post that said, "When you are in a difficult place, realize the Lord either placed you there or allowed you to be there for reasons perhaps known for now, only to Himself. The same God who led you in will lead you out." There were so many memes and images just like this. I could literally see God breathing into me, building me up with His strength through something we tend to think of as "not of God." He was using it in a way to get to me, even when I was trying to numb my mind.

We are to endure the pain of this life until such a time as God gives an answer to our prayers. The answer to my prayers came in eighteen days. At the time, God's clear answer was "my Grace is sufficient for you." But over time I realized his answer was also a resounding "No." I don't think I was ready to understand the implications of "No" at the time of Vinny's death so God gave me Grace instead. But now, in the wake of His answer, I will strive to patiently endure a lifetime until I can see my son's face again. Until I can hear his sweet voice or feel his body in the embrace of a sweet hug.

In Revelation, there is an amazing verse talking about a bowl of prayers:

> *"Each one had a harp, and they were holding golden bowls full of incense, which are the prayers of God's people." Revelation 5:8*

Pastor Paul of Calvary Church said it this way: "Verse eight continues, each holding a harp and golden bowls full of incense, which are the prayers of the saints. I also find it very comforting that the prayers of the saints don't just evaporate before God. They're kept, your prayers are kept before God. It's funny we pray about something and then we start feeling guilty because maybe we haven't prayed about it. It's kind of like our prayers went away… Ah, wish I'd have prayed more. You know what? God kept your prayer. It wasn't lost. It didn't go away. God's not hard of hearing and he didn't forget about what you prayed. I'm not suggesting that we shouldn't keep praying. The Bible tells us to keep praying. I'm just saying your prayers are kept and that's pretty beautiful."

The imagery of this was powerful to me. All of those prayers, even prayed once, are in front of God continuously. Where we are stuck in the limits of time, our one prayer could be sitting in the bowl before God for ten years and it's just as current for Him. The smell of the prayers is like sweet, sweet incense. I love this because sometimes I forget to pray. Praying is what we are called to do, to lay it all out at his feet. We are supposed to confide in God with our needs and wants, not because He doesn't know them or they are a surprise to Him, but because it fosters our personal relationship with Him. Just because I haven't gotten an answer now, doesn't mean that in ten years when I have forgotten all about that specific prayer or have moved on from it doesn't mean that God has. It's just as current to Him as the day we made it.

I have no choice but to wait patiently. To endure the pain of losing my Vinny because the answers to my questions won't come until the God of Heaven calls me home. The epitome of perseverance. But how many years will that be? And how are we to spend that time?

> *"Abraham breathed his last and died in a good old age, an old man and full of years, and was gathered to his people." Genesis 25:8*

> *"Abraham was 175 when he died. And he was 'full of years.' Isaac lived a hundred and eighty years. Then he breathed his last and died and was gathered to his people, old and full of years." Genesis 35: 28-29.*

Both times these men were described to have lived long lives "full of years." I think it's possible for us to endure long lives and miss out on the "full of years" part. The key is trusting that God is with you WHILE you patiently endure. I need to use this time to seek him. I need to say, I will endure and I will strive to do so patiently until such a time as God deems my work here done. I will pray that when the waiting feels like a two-hundred-pound brick sitting on my chest, that God sends a friend to help bear the weight. I will pray that God will infuse me with His peace and calm when it seems impossible. I don't have to like this path I'm on, but I was called to it and I will persevere.

> *"We glory in our sufferings, because we know that suffering produces perseverance; perseverance, character; and character, hope." Romans 5:3-4*

"Therefore I will boast all the more gladly about my weaknesses so that Christ's power may rest on me." This was the apostle Paul's take on the thorn in his side. The pain he had been given in his life. Maybe you are like my husband, and you have studied 2nd Corinthians 12 for years and so the understanding of God's grace and our weakness, and the ability to BOAST about that weakness, is clear and understandable for you. But then maybe you are more like me. The morning I stood there with Vinny was possibly the first time I had really ever heard that verse and it was less clear to me.

The understanding of God's Grace, an unmerited gift or undeserved favor, in its simplest meaning is clear enough. But this Grace, this Grace is different. Pastor Paul of CC Ontario says "This grace is the grace that ENABLES—this grace EMPOWERS us to do or to be ... and we cannot have access to this grace, until we are weak. Until we are dealt a hand of pain. Until we are an empty vessel and there is nothing left for us to do of our own accord. This is when the POWER of God's grace can fill us. "For when I am weak, then I am strong." For when we are empty and helpless and unable to take another step on our own, this grace then enables us, strengthens us for HIS purpose, not our own."

Don't we all find that when we can lift ourselves up and take another step from our strength, our own resolve, there is zero room for humility? This ultimately leaves no room for the grace of God and the wonderful things only His spirit can bring out of pain and hardship. Usually our own doing eventually crumbles, whether in days or years, and who do you turn to then?

The purpose of this grace, this weakness, and eventually strength is for God's Glory, not our own. God activated this grace in me. Months into "the after," my strong connection to the hospital, and my artistic mind, came together to form a small charity called One Small Seed. With God at the center, we made clay earrings to raise money for the families of sick children. There were so many ways in which God met me on that path. Am I sure that was the path He wanted me on? Maybe so for a time. But regardless, He met me there. In a few short months, we had raised over $30,000, all donated to families with children in the hospital.

Vinny's marigold bloom was our logo and the idea that one small seed can make a big change propelled us forward. Kim and a bunch of my ladies met together to help create the earrings and we did a lot of good out of it. There were nights that I would create batches and batches of earrings. People would often ask me, "When do you get all this done!!

Do you not sleep?" I believe this is where the power that enables came in. I could feel this drive, this energy propelling me forward. I wanted to do it! I "delighted" in the work, and I kept going until red tape started getting in the way.

In the back of my mind was this still, small voice. This is all great, but is this my true purpose? Is this the important part of what happened? I truly felt that God was telling me it was NOT about selling earrings, and donating to families however wonderful that was. It WAS about telling my story. The important part of what happened was God's presence through it all. Why show me all that He did if I was supposed to keep it to myself? The "work" I was doing was inherently good, but it was also another good distraction.

In obedience to what I believed God was telling me, I began to write, to "tell my story." Now you can search everywhere but you will NOT find another book from me! Writing isn't a craft I have honed, but over and over it says that God will give you what you need for a task he has called you to.

2 Corinthians 3:5 reminds us, "It is not that we think we are qualified to do anything on our own. Our qualification comes from God." Jesus said, "Go home to your own people and tell them how much the Lord has done for you, and how he has had mercy on you." Mark 5:19

God has shown my soul mercy in so many ways and there are so many stories in the Bible of God calling an unlikely or "unqualified" person to do something. Writing a book is something I am not particularly qualified for, but I decided to trust God, to walk in obedience, and let Him lead the way, wherever it may go.

A few years later, I met Benjamin for coffee. Our connection will always be tied to our time spent at Vinny's bedside for what I imagine to be the rest of my life. We were marked in some way, some invisible chain that links us all together. I asked him why, of all the patients he has seen, was our connection so strong? Why did our experience leave such a lasting impression? He said that besides his connection from his own childhood experience, he felt our conversations had a lot to do with it. My need as a mom for knowledge beyond the medical, about the people who surrounded us and their stories, and the "humanness" of our conversations led to a deeper bond. Even though as nurses they are taught to detach from patients in some ways, to not get too close, sometimes it's a natural occurrence. Or maybe even one made by God alone.

During our coffee time he shared a bit more information about his childhood trauma than he had before. Timing is everything, I guess. When he was blown out of that tree he remembers looking down at himself. Seeing himself hanging in that tree from above as if held by the waist by angels. He said even though there seemed to be a mist, colors were brighter and clearer than normal. And he felt peace. He had a distinct understanding that his life was over and he might be moving onto Heaven and it was okay. He could see people moving beneath the tree—the first responders, people that had been there in the past and possibly in the future. Hundreds of people were beneath the tree as he hovered above, surrounded by angels.

That was how he knew the children that passed on from his care were ok. They were held by the same peace he was. He knew they would experience the brightness and love he felt and they would no longer be limited to their suffering bodies or futures of pain and heartache. He'd had a firsthand near-death experience. God comes full circle doesn't He?

CHAPTER 19

JESUS BESIDE US

Lord, make me an instrument of your peace: where there is hatred, let me sow love; where there is injury, pardon; where there is doubt, faith; where there is despair, hope; where there is darkness, light; where there is sadness, joy.

—*Prayer of Francis of Assisi*

I have found myself standing in line at the grocery, holding my basket of purposefully selected items, thinking no one around me knows the darkness I feel. Here I am talking to a stranger with the normal niceties and they have no idea what I've been through. I walk around with a thorn forever in my side. I've contemplated, during our mundane conversations, "this person doesn't know that I just watched my son die. They can't see the torture I see behind my eyelids every night. Heck it's possible I might be vividly replaying the scenes at this very moment and I look just like everyone else."

Isn't that the point of it all? I notice the woman in front of me with the baby on her hip. How many babies did she lose before she could hold that precious gift? The man standing behind me ... did he just lose his job, his home, his family? Heck, I have close friends that have seen all sorts of nightmares. Cancer and lost limbs and accidents, death of loved ones, mothers, fathers, and friends. EVERYONE has been through and IS carrying something. As much as they can't see my pain, I can't see theirs either and out of that darkness flows compassion. How much does a kind word help me when I am struggling and the stranger in front of me has no idea. How much more can I give to the people around me? How many abuses have they suffered? I'll tell you the answer is likely many. How many lives have they lost? How many people have hurt them, discarded them, changed them. How many of the people standing around us have gotten up, scorch marks lining their insides, and continued on with life, carrying the pain that this unforgiving world has lashed out? How great is my pain, could theirs be even greater? How many of you reading this have mentally checked off every hardship I've just listed, because likely you can see, even those long away hurts, play out right before your eyes.

A kind smile and a nice word is not hiding the pain of what I've endured, but it's having compassion in the midst of it. Just the same way that God has compassion for our struggles.

> *"The Lord is gracious and full of compassion, slow to anger and great in mercy." Psalm 89:14.*

> *"But You, O Lord, are a God full of compassion, and gracious, longsuffering and abundant in mercy and truth." Psalm 86:15.*

> *"Shout for joy, you heavens; rejoice, you earth; burst into song, you mountains! For the LORD comforts his people and will have compassion on his afflicted ones." Isaiah 49:13*

In this life we are sure to have suffering. God shows us Grace in our pain and our trials and we should strive to give that same grace to others.

"Do not let any unwholesome talk come out of your mouths, but only what is helpful for building others up according to their needs, that it may benefit those who listen … Get rid of all bitterness, rage and anger, brawling and slander, along with every form of malice. Be kind and compassionate to one another, forgiving each other, just as in Christ God forgave you." Ephesians 4:29-32

One morning in Bible study, we were discussing what it would be like when we get to those pearly white gates and stand before God for the judgment. Did you know that if you choose to accept Jesus as your Lord and Savior here on Earth there will be no judgment for you? At that time Jesus will step in and say "She is mine! My blood has covered her sins and they are forgiven."

God gave me this sweet, sweet, thought, another small vision that flashed before my eyes, as we were discussing what it will be like to stand before God. As if I was standing in the clouds before the pearly white gates myself, waiting for my judgment, I saw Jesus come up next to me and before a word was said I was filled with this immense, exuberant love. It was as if I had waited my whole life to see this particular loved one and instead of waiting for Him to step in for me to say that my sins were forgiven and my salvation was granted, I jumped into His arms like I would a long-lost friend. Nothing else mattered in that moment because I was in the presence of Jesus. My friend. My savior. Can you imagine that? Experiencing an overwhelming feeling of being "home" as all the pain from this lifetime falls away? Can you imagine Jesus stepping in for you and calling you His friend? It's a moment I will cherish forever and I can't wait to experience it when the time comes.

The thing is, I believe Jesus wants us all to experience that moment. Every single one of us, all of His children, I think He wants us to jump into His arms the moment we get to be in His presence. Do you know Jesus in that way? Because I'm pretty sure that's how He knows you. Before any of this happened to me Jesus had it on my heart to show people that He is here with us. He's there with you. He's sitting on the bed, across from you at the desk, next to you in the chair right now watching you read these words. He's hoping that you will turn your head to the side and say "I can feel you with me Jesus. I believe that you died for me and one day I want to be with you for the rest of eternity." He was with you in the hospital room. He cried right next to you at the funeral. He was next to you during that dark time just waiting for you to call His name. He's hiding in the pantry with you while your children run amuck and you silently cry from being overwhelmed. He's saying I'm with you in the mundane disappointments in life, just the way He was with me in the depths of my despair.

How many times had I called out to God, "I need you God! Where are you! Help Me! I need to hear your voice. Show me a sign that you really are with me again and again." There have been so many times in my life that God has shown Himself and still, daily, I ask for more. I don't need to see more out of disbelief. I need more because I know the overwhelming comfort His presence brings. To know that God is with me gives me the strength I need to move forward another day. The wonderful thing is that every time I have asked for Him to show Himself, He hasn't replied with, "again? Wasn't all that enough? How many miracles must you see? How many times do you have to ask? Don't you know yet?" Instead, He graciously, patiently, and gently responds to my call. "Ask and you shall receive, knock and the door will be open to you, seek and you shall find. With the love of a father He says, "Here I am, I am with you. I have always been with you. I have always been beside you. Look to your right, I am there. Look to your left, I am there. I have been beside you in the past, and will be in the future. And after all that, when you still ask, I will answer."

So where was God when my child was dying? Right there next to me. Where was God when my world was falling apart and my heart was caving in? In the depths, right there with me, answering my call. The entire time. Even now, Jesus is sitting right there with you too. Watching you read this with love in His eyes and open arms. Waiting for you to see Him and welcome Him into your heart. All you have to do is ask.

EPILOGUE

*"See, I am doing a new thing! Now it springs up.
Do you not perceive it? I am making a way in
the wilderness and streams in the wasteland."*

Isaiah 43:19

There were times during "the After" that I would hear verses about God "restoring what the locusts have eaten." But I would think, "how could I get back what has been taken from me?" I will never again see my son's face or hear his laugh until I have passed from this world. Still, God makes us that promise. I decided that I didn't yet have the answer and maybe I would have faith in the words Pastor Furtick spoke before, "if it's not good, God's not done yet." I had faith that God would bring some small joy back into my life, at some point further down the road, I just wasn't sure how.

As I had mentioned before, Chris and I had always had a strong affinity for adoption. Ever since I was eighteen and we welcomed my cousin Lily into the family from China, and then Sophie again eight years later, I knew I would one day want to adopt. We had planned for it to be later on in life.

After Vinny passed, Chris and I had a serious conversation about what we wanted our family to look like. The plan we had made for our family was forever broken. We were happy to move forward with just the three of us if it was what God wanted. But we thought, since we weren't getting any younger, if we wanted to adopt we should start the process. It could take a long time. There are so many children in the world that are without a family and in my "Maraness" I wasn't about to bring another one into this crazy world, so we started the paperwork with the Department of Social Services in January of 2023. Our preference was to adopt a little girl between the ages of newborn to seven. As silly as it may seem, I had always identified as a "Boy Mom." I didn't want any confusion on who those two boys were. Plus having a girl would be new and it was always a dream of mine. It took months to get everything done and we were finally approved by the state of South Carolina at the beginning of September. All we had to do now was wait and see what God had in store.

Months went by with nothing more than a few inquiries and I kept thinking, this is in God's hands and God's time. Also, I remembered the saying, "My plan may look different than your preference. Have faith." We did our part and the rest was up to Him. We'd say, "Maybe she's not even born yet!" It was a busy season with Map Mom, and I really felt God wanted me to get this book on paper before we welcomed another child into the home. So I began to write. On January 12, 2024, I finished getting the last word down on paper. On Tuesday January 16, just four days later, we got a call from DSS. Unbeknownst to us, they had chosen our family to adopt a three-month-old baby girl! If we said yes to adopting her, they would bring her to us two days later!

We had not expected a baby. I always imagined she would be between the ages of three to seven. So many people wanted babies and we were open to an older child, so I just assumed she would be. Little did I know that God was giving me back the feeling of a little head on my chest. A feeling I had longed for, grieved, and even buried.

Not only was God faithful in delivering us a perfect, smiling baby girl, but she was well loved and perfectly healthy before she even arrived on our doorstep. When you adopt from foster care, most of these children experience immense trauma. We had prayed for her safety and happiness for a full year. We had prayed that whoever and wherever she was, a bubble was placed around her so that no harm could come to her while she waited. We also knew that whoever she was and whatever she had been through, we would love her as much as humanly possible. And now here she was, a perfect bubbly little girl with a smile that felt like sunshine. The blessing we have received from having her in our lives is more than I could have ever imagined.

Now does this replace or fix what happened to my Vinny? Absolutely not. He will always be my first born. He will always have left my arms too early and my joy in him won't be restored until I am in Heaven. But God sent us a new joy. A different joy. A joy that I wasn't sure I would ever feel again. We received the news of her one year and seven minutes to the time at which we announced we were submitting our papers. Same day, same hour, one year and seven minutes apart. If that wasn't enough of a sign from God, when she came, we found out her given middle name was the same as mine, even in spelling. Something that is usually handed down a family line. A true sign that she was to be part of OUR family.

While doing a project for work, I had been researching flowers of the month. There is a whole chart of flowers that represent each month of birth. When I looked up her birth month, the flower that represented her was none other than a marigold. Low and behold, the adoption was finalized the week of Mother's Day three years after I had received my first marigold. Some people say that coincidence is God's way of being anonymous. But when you have the Holy Spirit in your heart, it's like those coincidences are SHOUTS of God's goodness from the heavens, too bold to be misheard.

I want to thank her biological mother for delivering such a perfect baby girl. There are so many choices she could have made that would have changed the outcome. I thank her for giving this child a healthy start because she's a blessing. God has placed her in a home that will love and cherish her, for all of her days.

As far as calling me "Mara," God always knew my name, even in my bitterness and heartache, and He had the grace to bring me back to Kira.

WHAT NOW?

So what's next when you read something and it has left you with questions? Study. Ask the questions and then look for the answers. The places I have found answers to so many questions are listed below. Questions not just about grief but about life and how to live it.

What came before us? What is our purpose? Who is God and what kind of impact can He really have on my life? Substantial. With Him anything is possible and the best way to find out who He is is to learn about Him. The Bible is His manuscript for history and life. While it may be hard to understand, it should be the foundation for the truth you will learn about why we are here and ultimately what we are to do about it. These were the resources that helped me UNDERSTAND, in a more modern context, what those things mean. They help me see the black-and-white writings of the Bible in color and with explanation.

But ALWAYS have the Bible as your sounding board and basis for learning about Him. After all, those are HIS words.

Disclaimer: If you ever listen to a "resource," meaning a pastor's sermon, a video, another book, writing, etc. and have questions, or something in you wonders, "is that really right?" Trust that feeling and find out. We are called to Seek. The Bible will tell you if something someone has said is out of context or used incorrectly. You can find many "interpretations" or better yet "opinions" about what the Bible says but what it ACTUALLY says is most important. I have checked many times to find out a verse was only half quoted or taken completely out of context.

Online Resource: Pastor Paul Leboutillier Calvary Church Ontario. This is a full online series of sermons teaching every chapter in every book of the Bible. Pastor Paul goes line by line and explains what each concept means, how it was interpreted, what others say about it, and how to apply it to life today. This resource is beyond measure. I can put in my ear buds and listen while I paint. I often listen on long drives and it provides a wealth of information. If you have ever wanted to understand what the Bible is saying in a more simplified yet detailed way, his videos speak the truth. Now I don't know Pastor Paul. I have no reason to plug his free sermons other than they have had a dramatic impact on my knowledge of what's actually in the Bible without leaving me completely confused or, well, asleep. They are interesting and life-giving and while some of them may strike a chord, usually that is the Holy Spirit striking the chord about something you need to either change or research further to live a better life.

https://www.ccontario.com/

On their homepage, if you click on the tab that says Teaching and Resources, you will see a listing stating "Through the Bible with Pastor Paul." Once you click on that it brings you to a listing of every book in the Bible and you can choose chapter by chapter what you want to learn more about in whatever pattern you like. You can either watch the passage via YouTube or listen to the podcast. It is a great way to understand more about the Bible.

Book: *Imagine Heaven* **by John Burke.** As I said previously, this book helped me think about Heaven in a way I had never considered before. Including the question, "Does it really exist?" It will lead you to wanting to know more about Heaven and there are many more books available to research further. Again, Seek and you shall find. There are two other reasons I would recommend this book. First, I wish I had known these things BEFORE Vinny died. I could have spoken to him about them while he was in the hospital. I could have whispered them in his ear to prepare him for what I didn't even know was coming. We will all find ourselves at the deathbed of someone we love. To be able to offer them words of comfort and hope, when oftentimes there are no words, can bring peace when it is unlikely. The second reason is for you. When I think of Heaven now, I look to it with expectation and wonder instead of fear and confusion. I hope everyone finds that. When your day comes to be called from this world, I hope you can look to it with a peace that goes beyond comprehension. With the hope that what comes next will be better than what you are leaving. The way to find that peace and hope is to find Jesus in this life before you reach the next.

Online Resource: Pastor Steven Furtick from Elevation Church. Pastor Furtick offers weekly sermons that often have me feeling that familiar stirring that can only be the Holy Spirit. When I hear him speak, I know that God is using him. He offers short One Minute Messages on all social media platforms that can be followed easily. His church has more of a charismatic nature, which may or may not be your cup of tea, but regardless of the style, the message is clear and God is in it. I have used many of his quotes in this book because they impacted me when I needed it most. That, my friends, is God's timing. I don't know Pastor Furtick either! But God used his messages to speak to me in the most profound and personal way. It's God that does that and He can do that for you too.

Another great way to find God is to find a church. Join other people who are seeking Him. That's where all of my "resources" came from! Either from friends at church or in my small group; other men and women who wanted to know more about who Jesus is and why we are here. My home church is **Seacoast Church** in Mount Pleasant, South Carolina. They have fourteen small campuses in the Carolinas but reach to many countries online. They are working to translate the Bible into every language so that everyone, even those in the remote corners of the world, have the opportunity to read the gospel. We are proud to call them home. When you look for a church, know that you will find many different types of people and beliefs, but really it's God who you are looking for. Look for Him wherever you end up. If He isn't there, you may not want to be either.

These are the main resources that impact my life besides the actual Bible. But the Bible should always come first. Just like religion, people are changeable, but the Bible is not. God is not. We can be sure that He is steadfast and unwavering in His love for every single one of us.

HELPFUL BIBLE VERSES FOR GRIEF AND HOPE

Be strong and courageous. Do not be afraid or terrified because of them, for the Lord your God goes with you; he will never leave you nor forsake you. Deuteronomy 31:6

You will be secure, because there is hope; you will look about you and take your rest in safety. Job 11:18

At least there is hope for a tree: If it is cut down, it will sprout again, and its new shoots will not fail. Job 14:7

My eyes have grown dim with grief; my whole frame is but a shadow. Job 17:7

*But those who suffer he delivers in
their suffering; he speaks to them
in their affliction. Job 36:15*

*Have mercy on me, L*ORD*, for I
am faint; heal me, L*ORD*, for my
bones are in agony. Psalm 6:2*

*The boundary lines have fallen for me in
pleasant places; surely, I have a delightful
inheritance. I will praise the L*ORD*, who
counsels me; even at night my heart
instructs me. I keep my eyes always on
the L*ORD*. With him at my right hand,
I will not be shaken. Psalm 16:6-8*

*One thing I ask from the L*ORD*, this only
do I seek: that I may dwell in the house
of the L*ORD* all the days of my life, to
gaze on the beauty of the L*ORD* and to
seek him in his temple. Psalm 27:4*

*I love you, L*ORD*, my strength. The L*ORD*
is my rock, my fortress and my deliverer;*

*my God is my rock, in whom I take
refuge, my shield and the horn of my
salvation, my stronghold. Psalm 18:1-2*

*Be merciful to me, LORD, for I am in
distress; my eyes grow weak with sorrow, my
soul and body with grief. Psalm 31:9*

*Taste and see that the LORD is good; blessed is
the one who takes refuge in him. Psalm 34:8*

*The LORD is close to the brokenhearted
and saves those who are crushed
in spirit. Psalm 34:18*

*God is our refuge and strength, an ever-present
help in trouble. Therefore we will not fear,
though the earth give way and the mountains
fall into the heart of the sea, though its
waters roar and foam and the mountains
quake with their surging. Psalm 46:1-3*

*He says, "Be still, and know that I am
God; I will be exalted among the nations,*

I will be exalted in the earth." The LORD Almighty is with us; the God of Jacob is our fortress. Psalm 46:10-11

My flesh and my heart may fail, but God is the strength of my heart and my portion forever. Psalm 73:26

My eyes are dim with grief. I call to you, LORD, every day; I spread out my hands to you. Psalm 88:9

Give thanks to the LORD, for he is good, his love endures forever. Psalms 107:1

My comfort in my suffering is this: Your promise preserves my life. Psalm 119:50

Let the morning bring me word of your unfailing love, for I have put my trust in you. Show me the way I should go, for to you I entrust my life. Psalm 143:8

*He heals the brokenhearted and binds
up their wounds. Psalm 147:3*

Trust in the LORD *with all your heart and
lean not on your own understanding; in
all your ways submit to him, and he will
make your paths straight. Proverbs 3:5-6*

*Surely God is my salvation; I will trust
and not be afraid. The* LORD, *the* LORD
*himself, is my strength and my defense; he
has become my salvation. Isaiah 12:2*

*Do you not know? Have you not heard? The
LORD is the everlasting God, the Creator
of the ends of the earth. He will not grow
tired or weary, and his understanding no
one can fathom. He gives strength to the
weary and increases the power of the weak.
Even youths grow tired and weary, and
young men stumble and fall; but those who
hope in the* LORD *will renew their strength.
They will soar on wings like eagles; they*

will run and not grow weary, they will walk and not be faint. Isaiah 40:28-31

So do not fear, for I am with you; do not be dismayed, for I am your God. I will strengthen you and help you; I will uphold you with my righteous right hand. Isaiah 41:10

For I am the LORD your God who takes hold of your right hand and says to you, Do not fear; I will help you. Isaiah 41:13

When you pass through the waters, I will be with you; and when you pass through the rivers, they will not sweep over you. When you walk through the fire, you will not be burned; the flames will not set you ablaze. Isaiah 43:2

For I know the plans I have for you," declares the LORD, "plans to prosper you and not to harm you, plans to give you hope and a future. Jeremiah 29:11

Because of the LORD*'s great love we are not consumed, for his compassions never fail. They are new every morning; great is your faithfulness. Lamentations 3:22-23*

For he does not willingly bring affliction or grief to anyone. Lamentations 3:33

Blessed are those who mourn, for they will be comforted. Matthew 5:4

Come to me, all you who are weary and burdened, and I will give you rest. Take my yoke upon you and learn from me, for I am gentle and humble in heart, and you will find rest for your souls. For my yoke is easy and my burden is light. Matthew 11:28-30

He (Jesus) said to her, "Daughter, your faith has healed you. Go in peace and be freed from your suffering." Mark 5:34

Jesus looked at them and said, "With man this is impossible, but not with God; all things are possible with God." Mark 10:27

Peace I leave with you; my peace I give you. I do not give to you as the world gives. Do not let your hearts be troubled and do not be afraid. John 14:27

Jesus said to her, "I am the resurrection and the life. The one who believes in me will live, even though they die; and whoever lives by believing in me will never die. Do you believe this?" John 11:25-26

So with you: Now is your time of grief, but I will see you again and you will rejoice, and no one will take away your joy. John 16:22

I have told you these things, so that in me you may have peace. In this world you will have trouble. But take heart! I have overcome the world. John 16:33

*I consider that our present sufferings are
not worth comparing with the glory that
will be revealed in us. Romans 8:18*

*And we know that in all things God works for
the good of those who love him, who have been
called according to his purpose. Romans 8:28*

*For I am convinced that neither death nor
life, neither angels nor demons, neither
the present nor the future, nor any powers,
neither height nor depth, nor anything
else in all creation, will be able to separate
us from the love of God that is in Christ
Jesus our Lord. Romans 8:38-39*

*May the God of hope fill you with all joy
and peace as you trust in him, so that
you may overflow with hope by the power
of the Holy Spirit. Romans 15:13*

*Praise be to the God and Father of our Lord
Jesus Christ, the Father of compassion and
the God of all comfort, who comforts us in*

all our troubles, so that we can comfort those in any trouble with the comfort we ourselves receive from God. 2 Corinthians 1:3-4

Therefore, we do not lose heart. Though outwardly we are wasting away, yet inwardly we are being renewed day by day. For our light and momentary troubles are achieving for us an eternal glory that far outweighs them all. So we fix our eyes not on what is seen, but on what is unseen, since what is seen is temporary, but what is unseen is eternal. 2 Corinthians 4:16-18

I can do all this through him who gives me strength. Philippians 4:13

Therefore encourage one another and build each other up, just as in fact you are doing. 1 Thessalonians 5:11

Cast all your anxiety on him because he cares for you. 1 Peter 5:7

He will wipe every tear from their eyes. There will be no more death or mourning or crying or pain, for the old order of things has passed away. Revelation 21:4

ACKNOWLEDGMENTS

First and always, I want to thank Jesus for His grace and presence while writing this book. I cherish the moments I can feel your guidance and the motivation to keep pushing forward. This book is for you and all those who may walk a path of suffering. I pray that they will seek your face and, in the process, find a Father full of love and acceptance.

Second, I would like to thank doctors and nurses everywhere. I don't know how you walk next to children riddled with pain and disease. To bear the weight with them and offer them comfort in the process is something a mother could only dream of. Thank you for your diligence and consistency in showing up for your patients, even when your own life may be in disarray. It is truly selfless and you are our heroes.

Lastly, thank you to all of those who know us as a family. You gathered around us the way you hear about in fables. When they say it takes a village to raise a child they leave out the part where it also takes a village to walk through losing one. Your continued support and love has helped me through the most difficult, dark days of my life. I pray that anyone who has to walk the journey of suffering is surrounded by people as amazing as you are.

One day we will all be together again, in a bright, colorful, love-filled paradise celebrating with those we have lost too soon. You'll find me there, on streets of gold, walking with my son and praising the name of Jesus. Until then.

REFERENCES

Burke, John. *Imagine Heaven: Near-death Experiences, God's Promises, and the Exhilarating Future That Awaits You* Baker Books, 2015.

Holy Bible. New International Version, Zondervan Publishing House, 1984.

Stanley, Charles, Pastor. *Grace In Times of Trouble- Part 2.* In Touch Ministries. 2021. Radio Sermon.

Carnes, Codie. Jobe, Kari. Elevation Worship. *The Blessing.* Graves Into Gardens. 2020.

Building 429. *I Will Fear No More.* Fear No More EP. 2019.

Warren, Rick, Pastor. *Faith Produces Perseverance.* PastorRick.com. 2024.

Furtick, Steven, Pastor. *One Minute Messages.* Elevation Church. 2021.

C. S. Lewis. *Mere Christianity.* HarperCollins, 2009.

Perry, Sara. *365 Days of Prayer for Grief and Loss*. BroadStreet Publishing Group. 2020.

Alexander, Eben. M.D. *Proof of Heaven. A Neurosurgeon's Journey into the Afterlife*. Simon and Schuster Paperbacks. 2012.

McVea, Crystal. *Waking Up in Heaven*. Howard Books. 2013.

Prince, Dennis and Nolene. *Nine Days In Heaven*. RCM Publications. 2011.

Leboutillier, Paul, Pastor. Revelation 4 & 5. *A Throne and A Scroll*. CCOntario.com. Podcast. 2023.

Garrett, J. C. (1994). *The prayer of Francis of Assisi: A counselor's prayer*. Counseling and Values, 39(1), 73–76.